What Others are Sayin
Teacher Tom's Second

"*Teacher Tom's Second Book* has once again captured his profound understanding of children. His stories and insights are not only thought provoking, they are full of compassion, respect and hope. This is a must read for everyone who lives with, or works with our precious young children."

> ~ Maggie Dent, parenting and resilience educator, and author of *Saving our Children from our Chaotic World, Real Kids in an Unreal World, 9 Things,* and *Mothering our Boys*

"Teacher Tom is one of those rare beings who is able to really see and hear children for being the very ones that they are. His stunningly articulate writing puts into words what children the world over need us to know – that they are born to grow and we are here to honor them on that awe-inspiring journey."

> ~ Dr. Vanessa Lapointe, R. Psych., author of *Discipline Without Damage* and *Parenting Right from the Start*

"Childhood and the richness of play need advocates with a strong and passionate voice like never before. If you're seeking a clear understanding of who children are and how we can value them, then look no further than Teacher Tom - beyond inspirational..."

> ~ Greg Bottrill, author of *Can I Go And Play Now?*

"If you spend time with young children, you need *Teacher Tom's Second Book*. Dip into this collection of essays, stories, and parables whenever you need inspiration or an affirmation of the innate goodness of young human beings. You'll be delighted by Teacher Tom's emotional generosity, humor and insight, which come together in "Aha!" moments that both re-affirm and challenge some of our most deeply held beliefs about children and how they learn."

> ~ Dr. Laura Markham, author of *Peaceful Parent, Happy Kids*

"When Tom addresses a topic, early childhood educators pay attention – because they know he speaks from experience. But mostly, they know how deeply he cares for children. *Teacher Tom's Second Book* is filled with the wisdom and insights we've come to expect from him. As usual, he pulls no punches – and I, for one, am thrilled!"

> ~ Rae Pica, author of *What If Everybody Understood Child Development?*

"Teacher Tom's poignant blog posts first captivated me back in 2009. His heroic ability to speak the truth on the behalf of children ignited my own passion to share TimberNook with the world. This book is truly a gift for both parents and teachers alike."

> ~ Angela Hanscom, TimberNook founder & author of *Balanced and Barefoot*

"A treasure! Teacher Tom facilitates higher learning in his preschoolers by trusting these "experts" to show him the way. In this second book, Tom shares more insights from his interactions and observations of children, opening a window into their developing minds as they gain autonomy, confidence, and social intelligence."

~ Janet Lansbury, author of *No Bad Kids*

"Teacher Tom sees little children with his eyes wide open and helps us see them as fully formed, fascinating, thinking human beings worthy of our respect. He knows and shows that children teach themselves and that the job of educators is to provide the kinds of communities in which children can do that best. I recommend this book to everyone concerned with children and the future of humanity."

~ Peter Gray, Ph.D., Research Professor of Psychology and author of *Free to Learn: Why Unleashing the Instinct to Play Will Make Our Children Happier, More Self-Reliant, and Better Students for Life*

Teacher Tom's Second Book

Tom Hobson

Seattle, Washington
Portland, Oregon
Denver, Colorado
Vancouver, B.C.
Scottsdale, Arizona
Minneapolis, Minnesota

ISBN: 978-1-59849-286-6
ISBN: 978-1-59849-289-7 (two volume set)
Library of Congress Control Number: 2020905866

To order additional copies or for institutional orders:
teachertomsfirstbook.com
teachertomssecondbook.com
teachertomsblog.blogspot.com

Printed in the United States of America

Editor: Danielle Harvey

Requests for such permissions should be addressed to:

Peanut Butter Publishing
943 NE Boat Street
Seattle, Washington 98105 USA
206-860-4900
www.peanutbutterpublishing.com

This book is dedicated

to the children I have taught

and who have taught me.

Contents

Acknowledgements

Teacher Tom's Blog, like this book, is the product of collaboration. Nothing ever happens without everyone.

I must thank my wife, Jennifer, and daughter, Josephine, who are the two most important people in my life, and the reason I get out of bed in the morning.

I must thank Elliott Wolf, my publisher at Peanut Butter Publishing, who's been a friend for over three decades, and without whom I doubt I would have ever birthed one book, let alone two. I must also thank my editor at Peanut Butter Publishing, Danielle Harvey, who has made this book better in every way.

I must thank my dear friend Mindy Lehrman-Cameron for her invaluable design contribution.

I must thank my loyal and hugely supportive readers, the many teachers and parents who check in with the blog day after day, commenting, sharing, and encouraging me.

I must thank the hundreds of families who have entrusted me with their children.

And most importantly, I must thank the children who have played with me, who have loved me, and whom I have loved.

Foreword

In his Introduction, Teacher Tom recommends *not* sitting down and plowing through the book from cover to cover. I must respectfully disagree; for whether it was intentional on his part or some subconscious input from his muse, the order in which his stories are presented serve as a cardio workout for your early childhood heart and soul. There is a nice warm up with a bit of a push, a plateau, then back up again, and again, until you reach a peak where your heart is racing and you feel called to action. You are writing in the margins, connecting what he says to what you have heard before, thinking of specific colleagues who need to get their eyes on this section and that one too, being challenged to perhaps push yourself out of your ideological comfort zone yet also feeling support as you are surrounded by like-minded people who know that growth—personal, professional, emotional, physical— occasionally requires some discomfort. And, similar to a good cardio workout, he doesn't bring you all the way back to a calm and comfortable heart rate; no, instead, he leaves you just elevated enough that you are encouraged to go out and do something in response to the call to action he once again so masterfully evokes in his readers.

> ~ *Lisa Murphy, author, speaker, early childhood specialist, CEP & founder, Ooey Gooey, Inc.*

Introduction

How I Would Use This Book If I Were You (And I'm Not)

The unexamined life is not worth living. ~Socrates

The contents of this book were written over the course of years. They represent personal experiences and thoughts stemming from moments during my school days, things read, conversations, challenges, and successes. For over a decade now, I've arisen every weekday morning, started the coffee, then begun to write about whatever was on my mind. Often, my thoughts are rather doughy and scattered, more a matter of emotion or intuition than reason. It's through the process of writing that I figure things out. As the American writer Flannery O'Connor once said, "I write because I don't know what I think until I read what I say." Mark Twain and Stephen King have made similar statements. That is my process as well.

Habitual reflection is essential, not just as an early childhood educator, but as a human being living in a world full of other human beings. At the end of the day, there is always something spinning away in my brain: something I've done poorly, something I don't understand, something of which I'm proud. Often, it's little more than the vestiges of an emotion. I begin by writing something that I know to be true, followed by something else I know to be true, followed by something else I know to be true, paying special attention to where the truth is that I simply don't know. Sometimes the process leads me to knowing. Sometimes I find myself in a state of profoundly not knowing, at least not that day. As you will see in this book (as well as in *Teacher Tom's First Book*), there are some themes I come back to again and again, each time trying to find a perspective that helps me discover something new.

I invite you to approach this book in this same spirit. I would not recommend sitting down and plowing through it, but rather taking time after each chapter to reflect, either on your own or with friends and colleagues. I don't expect anyone to agree with everything I've written here, but I do hope to provoke you, to stimulate thought, to show you a perspective that you've perhaps not considered. The important thing is not that we agree, but that we engage in reflection and a dialogue together that includes the unique children we teach, their parents, their communities, and our own values in a way that allows us to get a little closer to the truth as it is for each of us.

There is no cookie-cutter way to teach, to parent, or to reflect. There are, of course, some universal truths, but most truth is of the situational variety, and the only way to get there is through regular, honest reflection.

Tom

Part One:
What We Do Best Together

1

What We Do Best Together

The penultimate day of our school year was followed by pizza on the playground with parents, grandparents, and siblings, then a "bridge ceremony" in which each child symbolically "crossed over" from preschool to kindergarten. It was a big emotional day, but it wasn't our last day of school together. I like for our actual final day to be as normal as possible because, after all, that's what we do best together.

And it was. We gathered on the playground as usual, played, bickered, and settled our differences. We invited one another with sentences beginning with "Let's..." We played games about superheroes and baby tigers. And we mixed up potions we called "toxic."

The only thing that really set this day apart from all the others is that I planned to take a moment to tell them that I have loved being their teacher, to say that I would miss them, to wish them well, and to thank them for being my best friends. As we gathered on the checkerboard rug for what we call circle time, I held my copy of Eve Bunting's *Little Bear's Little Boat*, the book I traditionally read to children before sending them home as newly minted kindergarteners. I had read it the day before, and I intended to use it as a jumping-off point for my message. If you don't know the story, the central metaphor is a bear cub who loves taking his little boat out on the lake to row and fish and dream, but, as is a little bear's destiny, he grows too big for his little boat and must finally give his boat to a younger bear. The story ends with big bear building a bigger boat for himself.

The children clustered on the rug as usual, sitting where and how they will. Before I could begin my remarks, however, one of the girls said, "I want to try sitting in an actual circle today. We call it circle time, but we never sit in a circle."

The kids decided to give it a go, and they all scooted to the edges of the rug. There was some discussion about whether we had formed a circle or a square, then I said, "I read this book to you yesterday..."

I was interrupted. "Hey, Teacher Tom, I figured that book out! You're the little boat and we're the little bears!"

Someone else chimed in, "No, this school is the little boat and kindergarten is the big boat."

We spent a few minutes talking about the metaphor around the inward-facing circle we had formed, talking to one another like best friends do, taking turns, sometimes raising hands, sometimes not.

After some time, I took the moment for my message, referring to the metaphor that they all seemed to grasp. I thanked them and told them I'd miss them.

A boy raised his hand in response. "I'm sad that I won't see my friends at school anymore. I wish I could come back to this school."

"Me too."

"Me too."

They sat looking around the circle at one another for a few seconds. In all my years of sending children off to the rest of their lives, I'd never experienced anything quite like this. There are always one or two sentimentalists in every group, but in this case, the moment seemed to have impacted them all.

One girl broke the silence, announcing, "I'm going to invite all of you to my birthday party."

We then went around the circle as they declared their

intentions to invite one another to birthdays and to make play dates, essentially swearing to be friends forever. One boy suggested, "I think we should meet in a park one day every week," an idea to which everyone agreed. I've often gotten emotional at this time of year, and there are always teary-eyed parents, but this was the first time I had ever witnessed a group of five-year-olds well up like this.

Then, just when I was expecting them to break into a collective sob, a girl shouted, "But there's good news! We all get to go to new schools. My school is really big! A lot bigger than this school!"

There was an explosion of cross-talk as the kids began excitedly telling us about their kindergarten plans.

Finally, by way of wrapping things up, I said, "So, we're all a little sad to be leaving our little boat behind for the little kids to use, but we're also excited about our new big boats. We made plans to keep being friends and to keep playing with each other and to go to each other's birthdays. I also want to invite all of you to come back and visit this little boat any time you want. Just tell your moms and dads and I'm sure they'll bring to you to visit. I'll be so happy if you do."

There was a pause then, before a girl answered me, "But, Teacher Tom, *you're* invited to my birthday too." And then I received invitations to all their birthday parties, forever, before we went back to playing together, doing the thing we do best.

"We Need to Take Those Jewels"

We make rules in our classroom, together, by consensus, and among the first agreements we come to each year is "No taking things from other people," an echo of the Biblical commandment to not steal. There are anthropologists who argue that prior to the advent of the Agricultural Revolution around 10,000 BC, there was no such thing as "stealing" because there was no such thing as property, but, I expect, the urge to snatch some rare or special thing from the hands of another, if only to take a closer look, was still an urge with which our hunter-gatherer ancestors needed to deal. And that's really what we're usually talking about in preschool. *Stealing* implies taking something with the intention of illicitly and selfishly transferring ownership, while *snatching* falls more into the category of uncontrollable curiosity.

Whatever the case, in our modern world, these two distinct urges get lumped together, especially in the minds of young children who, through their play, are forever attempting to tease out both personal and social meaning.

One day, a group of boys was huddled together in a corner of the playground they had "built" for themselves.

"Guys, guys, I got a plan. We need to take those jewels."

"What jewels?"

"Those guys, over there, they have a bucket of treasure, and we need it for our team."

They were referring to their friends, boys with whom they often play, but who were on this day playing separately. They had spent the previous half hour or so collecting small shiny objects in a bucket. They were bits and bobs that anyone could pick up from the ground around our place—florist marbles, beads, pieces of toy jewelry—but they had named it "treasure," and now it was this treasure that these other boys were scheming to make their own.

There were a few moments of intense conversation—quiet and secretive. I couldn't hear their words, but their intentions were clear: they were planning an incursion to wrest control of that bucket, which they were going to hide and hoard somewhere in their hideout. Before long, they attacked, running toward the boys with the treasure, whooping, making fierce faces, wielding sticks like weapons.

The boys with the treasure looked confused at first, backing away a bit.

"We're going to take your treasure!"

"No, you're not! It's our treasure!"

The moment was tense as the two sides stood face to face. These guys had often played fighting games together, but I knew these children, I had taught most of them for three years. Physical violence wasn't in the offing, even as their bodies, tense and aggressively posed, seemed to indicate it. It was a moment both real and pretend, this stand-off above the sand pit. I recall moments like this from my own childhood. I knew their hearts were racing. I knew that some of them were feeling that they were now in over their heads, that they didn't really want to "steal," but just to snatch, to see and feel and hold the treasure that these other boys had made from debris that had always been there.

It lasted a few seconds as everyone stood posed, then one of the attackers dropped to his knees, dropping out, and began running his fingers through the sand. Then one of the defenders backed away, turning his back. One by one by one I saw their shoulders drop as the tension left their bodies, leaving only two boys still standing in opposition to one another, while the others milled around, no longer part of the game.

"We're using this treasure!" the defender said forcefully. "You can use it when we're finished!"

"Okay," his friend answered from under his glowering brow, as if making a threat, "we will!"

And then it was over, the aspiring robbers returning to their base, apparently satisfied with waiting for their booty. Once more, the treasure collectors scoured the ground for sparkling items to add to their cache.

"I Want to Be the Littlest Baby"

A child psychologist friend once told me that he kept a doll house in his office, explaining that he could often learn more about a child while playing "family" with her than during any number of hours of traditional talk therapy. I'm no therapist, but I can certainly see the potential there.

"I'm this baby."
"I'm the mommy bunny."
"I'm a baby too."
"But I'm the littler baby."
"I want to be the littlest baby."

Just in how they choose their roles, there's a whole world of aspiration and query. Over the years, I've noted that more children want to play the "baby" role, the younger and more helpless the better. For a long time, I assumed that "mommy" was the power role, the one that went to the child with the strongest urge to be in control, but I know now, as every child knows who has ever lost her place in the family to a younger sibling, it's the baby who really wields the power. Their helplessness demands attention, and that's what the babies do in these games.

A group of our four- and five-year-olds had been playing "baby" games for most of the year, typically assuming the roles of baby tigers or baby polar bears or other types of baby animals. There were no mommies in these games, but rather owners who are forever wrestling those naughty babies back into their beds or cages or caves or homes in order to "keep them safe." I'm sure my child psychologist friend would have a field day with these games filled with misbehavior and compulsion, these games where the baby, no matter how it behaves, continues to be cared for and loved.

As a teacher, I don't *need* to know what it means: I simply need to understand that the children are engaged in experiments they have designed to answer their unique social-emotional questions. There was a time when I would drop to my knees in the midst of these games and assume the role of "middle" or "oldest" child, the roles that appeared to me to have the least power, then attempt to role model how one can assume power (or satisfaction or control or whatever) from this role. Or maybe I would take on another role, hoping to somehow "teach" a lesson through my behavior within the game. They were misguided efforts at best. I had taken over their game to answer questions they weren't asking, skewing their data, scuttling their journey, making it about my adult attempts at social-emotional engineering rather than their own purposeful and meaningful exploration of the real world as they experienced it.

Now, when the children play house, I simply listen, even when they say things that make me cringe, even when the mommies boss the babies or the babies behave like mini-tyrants, even when I notice that no one wants to be the middle or oldest child. It's not my job to know what it means, that's for them (and perhaps a future therapist) to know. Our job, as important adults in the lives of children, is to create the space, to step back, and to wonder.

Wants, Interests, and Needs

As an avid reader, I spent ten years almost exclusively reading the works of novelists like Charles Dickens and George Eliot and Charlotte Bronte and Thomas Hardy. I consider Jane Austen to be the greatest of them all; some say that *Emma* was the first truly Victorian novel. I find Anthony Trollope to be a bit thin and Robert Louis Stevenson to be underrated. I'll bet that I know more about these novels than any preschooler alive.

It's a boast that won't impress anyone, of course, because even the few preschoolers who are already reading are certainly not reading 150-year-old English fiction. In the same fashion, the typical American preschooler is far more expert than I on the works of Disney (at least since 1970). The same goes for things like *Minecraft* and *Star Wars*. Every human alive, including all the children, have areas of expertise in which their knowledge surpasses my own.

Of course, many, maybe even most, adults would assert that knowledge of the Victorian novel is of a superior sort, but they're not only wrong, they're missing the point. No one made me read those novels. I read them because I *wanted* to read them, because I was *interested*, because it was knowledge that I felt I *needed* (albeit for reasons I'm still not able to fully explain). Likewise, as a boy, I was variously absorbed with baseball cards, *Batman*, and *The Hardy Boys*, none of which were considered "serious" pursuits, yet I made myself an expert, nevertheless. Looking back from my perch as a middle-aged man, I can see that those baseball cards were an important part of my lifelong fascination with statistics, *Batman* influenced my sense of humor, and *The Hardy Boys* inspired me in my quest to be an independent young man. When those Victorian novels were being written, many very serious critics considered them a complete waste of time, at best, while some labeled them a dangerous influence on young minds, much in the way that Disney, *Minecraft*, and *Star Wars* are critiqued today. Perhaps history will prove the critics right, but then again, any one or all of those subject areas may become the Victorian novel of our grandchildren's grandchildren's generation. In other words, we'll never know, and to pretend to know is hubris.

When it comes to modern early years education, there is a kind of unofficial hierarchy of knowledge at work, with mathematics and literacy at the top. Subjects like science, history, literature, and the humanities fill out the second tier, with physical education and the arts (dance and theater in particular) occupying the basement. Yes, there are schools that emphasize things differently, but the point is that Disney isn't on there at all, nor is popular music or baseball cards or *Batman*. Instead, we have prepackaged knowledge capsules of "learning objectives" for kids to swallow. For many, it's a bitter medicine, one they would rather hide under their tongues to be spit out the moment they are no longer under adult supervision. That's the way it usually is with "knowledge" for which we have neither want nor interest nor need. Oh sure, hard-working teachers do their best to smooth that over by striving to persuade their protégés, and sometimes it works and the children come to embrace the adult-approved want, interest, or need, but more often than not, it's a struggle for everyone.

It should be obvious to everyone that education would be a lot easier if we simply let the children pursue their own interests. Then there would be no need for "teaching" at all, at least when it came to the acquisition of specific bits of knowledge like the Victorian novel or *Star Wars*, because everyone would be self-motivated, and nothing beats self-motivation. The main role of the "teacher" would then be to merely keep up with the kids and help them find the information or tools they need. I suppose it would also be nice if that teacher could play the role of coach, confidant, and cheerleader as well.

So what of the math and literacy? Would kids grow up ignorant of those things? Would any of them ever read a Victorian novel? What kind of jobs will they get with their encyclopedic knowledge of, say, Beyoncé, and little else? Good questions, all. I'll try to address them in order.

As things are now, math and literacy are treated as core subjects, yet in real life, for most of us, calculating and reading never stand at the center of our endeavors, but exist rather as tools that allow us to pursue those things for which we have want, interest, or need. My own experience with baseball cards is a case in point: I spent hundreds of hours ranking, ordering, and grouping my cards based on the lines and lines of statistics on the back. I came to an understanding of fractions and averages and percentages long before I came across them in a textbook. But it was never about math. It was about baseball. The math was just a tool I used to pursue something for which I had want, interest, and need.

Reading works the same way. I didn't read *all* of *The Hardy Boys* mysteries because I was working on reading skills, it was because I was acutely interested in these two brothers, my elders, but still boys, who were free to roam the world, having adventures without some grown-up telling them what they need to know and by when they need to know it. The only reason we believe that most humans must be "taught" to read (or do math or understand basic science) is that we've been using school to "teach" them to read for generations. It's a habit. Believe it or not, people learned to read long before we started teaching it in schools. The advent of the ability to mass-produce printed material is what really boosted modern literacy. It was the Internet of its day, full of information, ideas, and entertainment for which people had wants, interests, and needs. People were highly motivated to figure it out, and so they did. In today's terms, we would say that reading went viral. By the beginning of the American Revolution in 1776, literacy rates were about what they are today (even a bit higher), and they've pretty much stayed there ever since, whether we were teaching it in schools or not. Reading is just a tool we use to pursue something for which we have want, interest, or need, and most of us learn it because of that.

So no, I don't think kids would grow up ignorant of math or literacy or science or history. Indeed, I expect they would grow up to view these things as useful tools rather than study chores because they would have learned to use them in the context of something for which they had want, interest, or need.

As for the second question, most of them would probably *never* read a Victorian novel, but that's really no different than things are now. Sure, many of us have been forced to read one or two, but most of us will never in our lifetime voluntarily read another. This is true of much of what we "learn" in school because humans typically don't respond well to being told what to learn because, to borrow from the eternal complaint of the sixth grader, most of it is "irrelevant." It is information for which we have no want, interest, or need, so we forget it as quickly as we can, freeing our brains for more important stuff.

And to reply to the third question about how being an expert on Beyoncé (or Disney or baseball card stats) helps you "get a job," my response is that it might. Maybe the skills we acquire researching our pop idols will serve us economically. It's far less likely that the historical dates we were compelled to memorize will help fill the coffers. Maybe the knowledge we gain about how the entertainment business works will give us a leg up. Maybe our fan participation in Beyoncé's social media marketing outreach will allow us to understand how marketing works. All of which might be useful when it comes to earning a greasy buck, but for me, that's kind of beside the point. If the primary purpose of education is to train future employees, then I say let's give the whole project up and let the corporations train their own damn workers.

I hope we all, first and foremost, want our children to be educated in the art of self-governance, and while part of that may be vocational learning, it is far from the primary goal. That is the promise and demand of democracy. And there is nothing more fundamental than the freedom to pursue one's own wants, interests, and needs, because that's how we find our own place amongst our fellow self-governing citizens. That is the pursuit of happiness, and it always runs through our own unique wants, interests, and needs.

"Only Little Dinosaurs Can Come into Our House"

The kids were playing with our regulation issue wooden unit blocks and our full collection of dinosaurs, both large and small scale. The idea, of course, was that the kids will build things and find ways to incorporate the dinos, but from the moment class started, a group of rowdy boys took over the area, and the game they chose was to empty the block shelves, dump the dino box, and race around kicking whatever was on the floor. It was a loud game, with lots of wild laughing, periodic shrieking, and occasional forays into wrestling or variations on the wrestling theme. Their play was interrupted regularly by angry flare-ups that sometimes included hitting, pushing, and tears, only to revert to form moments later.

It was the sort of thing that had been happening almost daily, and it kept the adults busy. On the one hand, we are a play-based school, which means the children lead, and it's not our place to put the kibosh on their self-selected pursuits. On the other hand, we're also responsible for their safety, both physical and emotional, so we were performing a balancing act between letting them do what they need to do while preventing them from killing one another or someone else.

This is important play for these kids. I see it for what it is: young people enthusiastically reaching out to other young people in friendship. As they get older, they'll have "better" ideas for how to play together, but for now it's exciting enough to just *be* together and to get a little crazy. It's enough to kick through the blocks and dinos, looking into one another's faces, and laughing like the Joker. Indeed, the excitement of being together is so palpable, so present among them on days like this one, that it's probably all they *can* do. Their love for one another is overwhelming.

That said, when they engage in this sort of play, they effectively shut down a part of the classroom to the other kids who are more inclined to, say, build things and find ways to incorporate the dinos. On this particular day, I was sitting on a bench monitoring the rowdy play when I was joined by Lois and Jane, a couple of girls who have older brothers. They sat with me on the bench, watching the boys.

Lois said, "Those boys are too dangerous. They're too crazy." She wasn't saying it as a complaint as much as a bemused observation.

I answered, "That's why I'm sitting way over here. I don't want to get hit by a block."

Meanwhile, Jane jumped off the bench and retrieved a couple stray dinos. "This is a mommy and a baby," she told us.

Lois waited until she saw a break in the action, dashed in for her own mommy and baby, then dashed back out, literally ducking her head. It didn't seem right that they had to risk their own safety (even if they only perceived they were at risk) to play with the toys in their own classroom. For better or worse, I decided to take action.

I retrieved my own mommy and baby, then said, "I've got an idea. Let's build a house for our dinosaurs!"

They liked the idea, so I gathered up a few blocks, then sprawled my large adult body onto the carpet, sort of commandeering about of a quarter of the area, creating a space for our building. I loudly declared, "We're building a house for our dinosaurs." When the rowdy play got near us, I said things like, "Hey! You almost hit me with that block," or "This is our dinosaur house!"

Before long, the boys had figured out the new boundaries for their game. And shortly thereafter, we were joined by a pair of kids, a boy and a girl, who do not have older siblings at home, kids who had previously been too intimidated by the rowdy play to even come as close as the bench on which we'd been sitting. Soon we had a nice little game of dino housekeeping underway.

In fact, our play began to attract the attention of the rowdy boys, one of whom knelt down with us, his two large T-Rex models poised, it appeared, to "stomp" our house. I said, "This is our house. We're not playing a stomping game. We're playing a quiet, gentle game."

He looked at me with a face full of the genuineness. "Why?"

"I guess we just don't want to be rowdy." This seemed to completely perplex him.

Then he asked, "Can my dinosaurs come into your house?"

Lois said, "No, they're too big. They'll smash it down."

Jane added, "Yeah, only little dinosaurs can come into our house."

He backed off a bit, unwilling to relinquish his big dinos, but remained where he could watch us. It wasn't long before he was joined by first one, then two more of his buddies, all holding their large dinosaurs. They formed an outer circle of kibitzers around our inside core of "gentle" players. It was as if we had a bubble around us. As we played, both the inner and outer groups grew, with more and more kids dropping down to join us, either contributing to our building or our dino family, while one at a time the rowdy players came to watch, all of them two-fisting larger dinosaurs.

As new kids joined us, I repeated, "This is our house.

We're not playing a stomping game," a mantra that was taken up by Lois and Jane. After a few minutes, I slowly extracted myself, leaving behind a corner of space for building things and incorporating the dinos. On the following day, the quiet, gentle corner emerged all on its own.

Unselfish

A young friend of mine who I've known for the entirety of her five years, brought me a gift. It was a picture she had drawn of me along with a message written in her own hand: "Ila (hearts) Teacher Tom." I probably receive a couple of these a week, pictures or other handmade gifts from the children I teach. They are often grubby, wrinkled, and torn from the effort of creation, and as I talk with the children, I always learn that every little mark or doodle has a story behind it.

Some time ago, I found myself in a friendly debate with a professional whom I hold in high esteem. He argued that young children are essentially selfish. Not that he was judging them, but rather, he believed, the ability to view the world unselfishly was a developmental stage that most preschoolers had not reached.

I've not found that to be true. Certainly, young children can be selfish, just like any of us, and some of them tend to be more selfish than others, but every day, all around me, I see young children disproving my esteemed colleague's theory. What I do see are children objecting to being told what to do. I see them sulking when commanded into sharing. I see them reacting angrily, sometimes even violently, to having something snatched from their hands, but, almost without fail, when a child *asks* for a portion or a turn, they receive it, usually gladly. Every day, I bring conflicts to an end, or even nip them in the bud, by simply pointing out, for instance, "Eleanor doesn't have any play-dough," a piece of information that a young child might not have discerned on her own, but that once clearly stated will respond by generously breaking off a piece of her own play-dough for the child who has none. In the lead up to the December holidays, I've discovered that children are at least as excited about the gifts they are giving as those they are about to receive.

If "selfishness" is acting without consideration of others for one's own personal profit or benefit, then "unselfishness" is sitting down with a piece of paper and a marker and spending time creating a gift. I would have to be incredibly selfish myself to not see the generosity in Ila's picture. She labored over those letters, shaping them carefully, for me, considering my feelings as she did. She reflected on my physical appearance, drawing a portrait, for me, that included the blue jeans I wear every day, my glasses, and a shirt she has seen me wear many times. As she presented the picture to me, I learned that she had wanted to get the color of my eyes right and was disappointed that she had guessed green instead of blue. This picture was not for her own personal profit or benefit, but for mine, one created expressly and thoughtfully for me. If that is not an example of unselfishness, then I don't know what is.

Ila gave me the picture on the playground, so after we had discussed it, I folded it up to fit into my jacket pocket. She had put so much unselfish thought into this gift, and it made me feel exactly as she had hoped, I expect, loved and treasured. Several times over the following days, I felt the paper in my pocket, wondered what it was, then opened it to find that it made me feel loved and treasured all over again.

Protection Play

I typically sit on the sign-in table near the front gate as the children in our afternoon class convene on the playground. This gives me a chance to greet each kid. Many give me a quick "hi" before running off to join their friends, but there are always some who need to start their day by bending my ear over something that has happened since the last time we saw one another, like a haircut or grandma's impending visit or a movie that impressed them. Some don't have anything particular to say but just seem to like some time with me by way of transition.

I try to not have any agenda throughout the *entire* day beyond the barest one of keeping the children relatively unharmed and playing, but during this particular time of our day together, after I've already done my work of getting ready, I am especially agenda-free, so it's a great time for just hanging out and shooting the breeze with whichever kids choose to linger.

One day, a boy who normally does not stop to chat with me, one who is usually running full speed with a stick in his hand, pretending with his friends to be action characters of some sort, declared that he was going to "protect" me.

I said, "That might be nice."

He wrangled a step stool into place and parked himself directly in front of me, stick-sword at the ready.

"I like being protected," I told him. "It makes me feel safe."

He was doing a pretty good job too, although, in all honesty, no one had yet tested his protective abilities. I was actually kind of curious what would happen if another kid did approach me, because although this boy likes playing action games, he is not prone to actual violence.

He smiled at me quickly, but he seemed to feel that his job was to sit still, surveying the grounds. Indeed, I don't think I'd ever seen him sit still for this long, and I've been his teacher for three years.

Soon, with few intruders to fend off, he grew restless. "I'm going to get some..." He didn't finish his sentence, but he returned moments later with a pair of chairs that he carefully arranged on either side of his stool. It was unclear whether they were intended as some sort of barrier or as invitations for others, but the arrangement was precise, something I discovered by inadvertently kicking the stool out of alignment, for which I was briefly scolded.

It was at about this time that we were approached by a boy with something to say to me. I cautioned him, pointing at my guard, "He is protecting me."

Before he could respond, my protector was on his feet, perfectly balanced like a martial arts master, posed defensively as if to say with his body, *Not one step closer, buddy!*

Unintimidated, the boy came closer, which caused my protector to execute a series of moves that looked like something from a Bruce Lee movie, high kicks and all. The fact that he did this in such close quarters without actually making contact, intentional or otherwise, was impressive.

I said, "Thank you for protecting me," before engaging with the boy, still unfazed, who had something to tell me.

I think we're often too quick to label action play as "aggressive" or "violent," when in fact it is actually this, protection play. I'll never forget last year when a girl complained about the "super heroes," telling us that they scared her. The superheroes were genuinely shocked to hear this. "But we're superheroes," one of them said in disbelief. "We *save* people!" So yes, while there may be some pretend aggression or violence, for most kids, most of the time, this is what it's about: playing at protecting the rest of us from evil. And yes, sometimes there are "bad guys," which are a necessary part of these sorts of games, just as there must be babies when we play at being mommies.

Before long, kids had joined the protective order by filling the chairs on either side of my original protector. They all sat there together between the world and me for quite a long time. Indeed, they were still there, protecting me, even when my adult agenda finally called me away.

A Wall to "Keep Others Out"

The two of them, a boy and a girl, built a wall. They had the entire constructive play area to themselves, all the baby-wipe box blocks to themselves, and they decided together to build a wall to, in their words, "keep the others out."

The goal was to build it so high that "no one could get over," and for quite some time, no one even tried. They used all the blocks to close off the entire space.

A classmate finally came to examine the wall.

"It's a wall to keep people out," they said, "but you can step over it and come in." When that first friend accidentally kicked down part of the wall in the process, they decided they needed a door.

More friends joined them, using the door in the wall built to keep the others out. Soon there were a half dozen of them inside the wall. Someone said, "This is our new play area."

There were no other toys in the walled play area, and the blocks were all incorporated into the wall. All they had was one another, the space, and that wall that was not really keeping anyone out.

They decided to make it a place for dancing. I put on some West African marimba music. They danced within the wall in their own spaces and in their own styles.

One boy found a box full of small, plastic rainbow-colored people and brought it inside the wall. He began arranging them along the top of the wall saying, "These people are our audience." Some of the kids helped him arrange the rainbow audience while the others danced.

As is usually the case with four- and five-year-olds, it isn't enough to play together without also touching one another. The dancers danced together until it evolved into a kind of pig pile under which one of them was trapped. She didn't cry, but they saw pain in her face and decided to play more gently.

Amazingly, after a good forty-five minutes, the wall with its precariously balanced rainbow audience was still standing. By now there was at least a dozen kids inside the wall that had been built to keep the others out, the wall into which they had built a door, a wall inside which they had danced and grappled and empathized and compromised.

Then, as is every wall's destiny, they kicked it over with such an eruptive suddenness that it alarmed us all. I had walked away just prior to that moment and returned, worried that they would somehow need big, responsible adult me in the aftermath of that wall coming down, but I saw only smiles on beet-red faces as they made rubble of that wall that could no longer even pretend to keep anyone out.

Moments later, a cry went up, "Let's build a tower!" And together they did.

Anarchists, in the Best Sense of That Word

Young children are the masters of fairness, although it may not always look like what we adults think of as fairness.

We've all heard kids complain, "It's not fair!" when they're told they must, for instance, wait their turn or share their cupcake. Adults might be inclined to attempt to correct them, but I will assert that the unfairness they perceive in those circumstances has far more to do with the adults *compelling* them to wait or share than the actual waiting or sharing. It's our knee-jerk adult idea that selfishness is the default setting that prevents us from seeing that.

When I sit down at our play-dough table, there are often a half dozen kids playing with this limited resource. One of them almost invariably has the lion's share. When subsequent children approach, they often say, "I need some play-dough." If the adults don't intervene, I've noticed that nine times out of ten, the child with excess will pinch off a handful and hand it over, expecting neither praise nor thanks. They might not do it as quickly as the adult would like, but that's because they are not reacting to a command, but rather considering a request, and that takes more time. Adults too often label that pause as selfish reluctance, when in reality it's the time children need to understand the situation and then do their own thinking: *She wants some play-dough. I have a lot of play-dough. I could give her some of my play-dough.*

When a child is using the swing and another child says, "I want a turn," if the adults don't intervene with their ideas about fairness, such as "setting a timer" or "counting," the child on the swing almost always gives way within a matter of minutes: *He wants a turn on the swing. I have been swinging for a while. I could give him a turn.*

I often wonder how we adults got this way, lacking faith in our fellow humans to share, take turns, and generally behave fairly without commands or rules or systems. Indeed, we act as if selfishness is baked into humans, as if our natural condition is "every man for himself," each vying against the other for advantages. But we're wrong. Anthropologists tell us that there is little evidence that our hunter-gatherer ancestors (99 percent of human existence) viewed fairness as something that needed to be imposed, and because of that, there was no need for any sort of hierarchy to control the behavior of others. Indeed, their social contract with one another seems to have operated more along the lines of what we today would call "anarchy," in the best sense of that word.

It wasn't until we gave up our hunter-gatherer ways in favor of the settled agrarian life that we invented the notion of "ownership" and discovered the need for commands, rules, and systems. Ownership was something that must be protected, and others must be made, one way or another, to labor for the benefit of the owner. In the process of inventing property, we also invented selfishness.

It's my assertion that humans are born as hunter-gatherer style anarchists, which is why they have no problem with defining justness in ways other than we do as adults. They know in their genes that it's unjust when those with more do not share with those who have less. They know that it is unjust when one person enslaves another, be it with chains or wages. They know that it is unjust when one person gets to "use" the labor of another. They know it is unjust when one person gets to tell another person what to do. Of course, they can't put this into words, but I've seen it time and again in how they treat one another when left to think for themselves.

We, however, have been taught that selfishness is the default setting for not just children, but all human beings. We don't trust their instincts, so we preemptively turn to commands, rules, and hierarchy, which, sadly, teaches children the very selfishness we seek to avoid. Meanwhile, when left to their own devices, children play together as anarchists, in the best sense of that word.

Putting Away the Blocks

We don't tell the children at Woodland Park that they must take part when it's time to tidy up the place, but most of them, most days, do.

I signal that it's clean-up time by banging my drum, then the adults start making informative statements:

"It's clean-up time."

"The blocks go in these orange boxes."

"I see a block on the floor."

The power of informational statements is that instead of commanding children (e.g., "Pick up the blocks," "Put them in the orange box," "Stop playing, please"), we create a space in which children can think for themselves instead of just react: *It's clean-up time. There's a block on the floor. I can pick it up and put it away.* When we command, even if we add the word "please" at the end, we leave children with only two choices, obey or disobey, while when we simply make statements of fact, we greatly increase the odds that any individual child will make his or her own decision to participate.

The most powerful version of the informative statements, I've learned, is to start naming names:

"I see Claudio putting away a long block."

"Sara and Monica are carrying a block together."

"Wow, Arnold is carrying five blocks!"

One day, I was making these sorts of informative statements as the two-year-olds were packing away some large blocks. One of the children was carrying a block atop her head.

I said, "Amy is carrying a block on top of her head."

Within seconds, nearly all her classmates had their own blocks atop their heads, each making eye contact with me as they passed on the way to the boxes in which we were temporarily storing them, waiting to hear their own names, so I obliged: "Claudio is carrying a long block on his head, "Sara is carrying a small block on her head," "Monica is carrying a medium block on her head," "Arnold is carrying five blocks on his head…"

It was not the most efficient way to put away blocks, but that's hardly the point. When we were done, the kids then turned to the stuffed animals of their own accord, eager to keep carrying stuff on their heads, so I just went right on narrating the story of "us" I saw unfolding before me.

I Am the Boss of Me

One day, a boy commanded me to do this or that, and I responded, "Hey, you're not the boss of me."

He replied, "I *am* the boss of you!" He intended it as a joke. Being a knee-jerk contrarian is where his sense of humor stood in those days. His smile told me he was anticipating an argumentative response.

I obliged by saying, "You are not the boss of me."

"I am the boss of you."

"No," I corrected him, pointing comically at his chest, "*you* are the boss of you," then at my own chest, "and I'm the boss of me." We went back and forth a bit, but then I switched things up by saying, "I'm the boss of you," to which he immediately responded, "No, I'm the boss of me and you're the boss of you."

The iconic performer Patti Smith once said, "No one tells me what to do anymore, except my daughter," a line that passes through my head each time a child attempts to boss me around. There's a part of me that's always tempted to treat them all like my own child, of course, relenting in the name of love with an understanding that they don't *mean* to command me, that it's just a childish shortcut, but I don't. Instead, I hold my ground, sometimes adding in the spirit of Ms. Smith, and say, "What do I look like, your mom?"

I say it first of all because it's true, but secondly, I want to role model the stance that I would like to see all people be able to take toward the world: *I'm the boss of me. You're the boss of you.* I try to not say it with jerk-ish defiance, but rather as a statement of fact. If children know me well, I'm confident that they already know that they can usually get what they want from me by simply converting their command into a question. When it's a younger child or one I've only recently met, I generally add, "But if you *ask* me, I'll probably do what you want me to do."

There are some adults who recoil at this approach, certain that I'm teaching the children to be disrespectful and disobedient, and they're half right. We are raising our kids to one day be adults in a democratic society, one in which we must be equal members if it is to work. We may as individuals choose to take a job or join a church or create other relationships in which we assume a subservient role, but the key concept is that it is a *choice* we make as free humans, one we should be able to quit the moment we find ourselves the victims of the abuse of power. The degree to which we don't have a choice about this is the degree to which we are not free.

As a middle-aged, white male, this is an easier stance to take than it is for others. The cards are clearly stacked in my favor, which is why I am particularly motivated to do what I can to ensure the children I teach grow up knowing that obedience, especially to me, is not required. I must earn their cooperation by cooperating with them the way I do with my fellow free adults. So yes, I am teaching children to be disobedient, at least to me, and I do so joyfully, but I hope, at the same time, I'm teaching them how to stand up for themselves on a day-to-day basis without being disagreeable. I want them to know that conversations about power, and particularly the balance of power, are not just acceptable, but necessary, be it based on age, sex, race, or socioeconomic status, and those conversations are most productive when they are done directly, calmly, and with the focus on finding ways to agree, because, after all, when obedience is removed from the equation, we are left with only our agreements.

And agreements among free humans are sacred.

Putting What They Had Learned to Use

We arrived one Monday morning in January to find that someone had rudely used our parking lot to dispose of their Christmas trees, a pair of noble firs.

The trees, naturally, evoked memories of the recent holiday, with children being inspired to share about their own trees, their decorations, their gifts, their relatives, their family traditions, and the ultimate fate of their own trees, some of which were still standing in their living rooms. We had obviously talked about a lot of those things in the run-up to the big day, and it was interesting to hear the differences between what they had anticipated and what had actually transpired. In other words, these illegally discarded trees showed me a snapshot of some of what the children had actually learned about their families and the holiday. They had previously expressed their theories about what was to come, and now I was hearing what had actually transpired, kind of like a pre- and post-test without, you know, the intrusive irrelevance and stress of an actual test.

The conversation then turned to whether or not the trees were alive. After some debate, they came around to the consensus that they were dead, despite the still-green needles, because they no longer had roots. But could they plant it and make it come back to life? That question generated more disagreement, with most coming around to the reality that these trees would never grow again, just as the ones that had decorated their homes would never grow again.

But that didn't mean they weren't going to try, if only to attempt to prove themselves wrong the way real scientists do. They began by choosing a spot, then digging a hole. They had no problem making their hole deep enough for a trunk, but with all those diggers, it turned out to be far wider than it was deep, which, of course, meant the tree would not stand on its own.

Someone said, "We have to dig a *down* hole, not an *out* hole," a description that needed no further explanation, although it took them some trial and error to figure out that digging such a hole is a one-person job.

Even so, once the "down" hole was dug, the tree wouldn't stand on its own, so as one boy held the tree, the others bent their backs to the task of backfilling around the trunk, then packing the sand down. When the boy holding the tree ceremoniously let go, the tree remained standing, provoking impromptu cheering. Then, employing more of the Christmas tree knowledge they had acquired over the holiday break, they went back and forth about whether or not it was "straight," looking at it from various angles, then adjusting it accordingly.

When they were done, someone said, "We have to decorate it."

"But we don't have any ornaments."

One of the diggers hung his shovel from a branch. "That could be our ornament." So the kids finished by decorating the tree with whatever wasn't nailed down.

They had learned about Christmas trees over the break, adding to the knowledge they had been accumulating on the subject over the course of their five years on the planet. They were motivated, sociable, and worked well together, testing their theories, putting what they had learned to use in the real world. And when they stepped back, they had done it: they had their very own decorated tree around which to celebrate.

Doing a Little Deep Democracy

I was hanging out on one of our swings, chewing the fat with some of the kids. I can't remember what we were talking about, but I said, "I guess I forgot," to which Roko earnestly replied, "You know, Teacher Tom, when you get older, you forget more stuff."

The following day, I was a sitting in a circle of children heartlessly arguing about *Star Wars*. Roko was there, and when one of the other kids insisted I was wrong about some detail, I answered, "Well, I saw the first movie a long time ago, when I was a teenager. Roko told me that when you get older, you forget more stuff, so maybe I just forgot."

Roko nodded. "It's true."

Cecelia didn't agree. "No, the way it works is you go to another school and another school, and every time you go to another school, you get smarter and you remember more."

Paul had another thought. "If you see *Star Wars* when you're little and short, then you get tall and old and you forget."

Roko's older brother Matija said, "When you get to be like seventy years old, you start to forget things. That's what's happening to my grandpa." Now I understood what Roko had originally been trying to warn me about.

Henry then insisted, "You get smarter when you watch TV."

I couldn't help myself. "Really?"

He clarified, "When you watch animal shows, then you get smarter...about animals."

Myla jumped in. "I'm a girl scout. We get badges when we learn new things."

Liam told us that he was going to be a boy scout.

One of the youngest boys said, "I'm going to be a girl

scout when I get bigger." Some of the older kids jumped on that, telling him that he was a boy and that he would have to be a boy scout.

He looked crushed, so I tried to buck him up by siding with him. "When I get bigger, I'm going to be a girl scout too. I want to get some of those badges so I don't forget so much stuff." When the kids then turned to me to insist that 1) I wasn't a girl and 2) I was already too old, I role modeled standing up for myself. "If I want to be a girl scout, I can be a girl scout."

Myla asked, "Are you like a girl inside of a man?"

"Maybe so."

"Does that mean you have a penis and a vulva?" She was joking, going for an absurdity.

Cecelia jumped in. "I know a girl with a penis."

Several of the older kids responded with some version of "Really?" an invitation to tell them more, unlike my earlier "Really?" to Henry, which had been, frankly, a good-natured but still judgmental expression of doubt.

"Yes, she has a penis, and she wants to be called *they*."

I asked, "She wants to be called *they* instead of *he* or *she*?"

"Yeah, so I call her... I mean, I call they *they*."

Myla asked, "So could they be a girl scout *or* boy scout?"

Cecelia shrugged. "I guess so. They can be anything they want."

Hanging around together, discussing the world and the people we find there, tossing out our thoughts and ideas, sharing without judgment, asking questions, learning new stuff, changing our minds: this is deep democracy.

Turning "Me" into "We"

"We need to move this bench." She said it out of the blue to no one in particular. It was a piece of furniture made from wrought iron and wood, so not by any means light-weight. Not only that, but it had been in the same spot for months. She began to wrestle with the bench as the rest of us watched her.

After a few seconds, two other girls joined her. Together they were able to wrest it from its position and lift it off the ground.

The instigator said, "We need to move this bench up there." She pointed vaguely toward the top of the playground, indicating an area near the gate. Without speaking, they began to shuffle in that direction. As they did, another girl joined them. Now there were four of them wrestling with the bench.

It was an unwieldy process. It wasn't the weight, which was something the four of them could easily manage, but rather the awkwardness of coordinating four sets of feet.

"We need to rest," their leader said, and with that they put the bench down. After a minute or so, she again said, "We need to move this bench," and together they lifted it, this time joined by yet another girl choosing to be included in her "we." They shuffled up the hill until they came to the top. There was some discussion now about exactly where the bench should go.

"We should put it here."

"No, we should put it over there a little more."

"Maybe we can move it back a little."

Once they had decided on the spot, the girl who started it all said excitedly, "Now we can sit on it!"

It's not magic, of course, but it always strikes me that way when young children begin to discover the power of turning "me" into "we."

A Rule That Stands Above the Golden One

They tell me that the Golden Rule is the only one we need, that every major religion has some version of it embedded in its theology, and it's a good one, the most familiar iteration being "Do unto others as you would have them do unto you." But it's not the highest rule. In my book, that honor goes to a rule that the kids agreed to among themselves a few years back: "Don't do anything to anybody unless you ask them first."

The Golden Rule doesn't ask for consent, it just asks each individual to look inward and assume that others feel as we do, while the kids' rule caused us to turn our attentions outward and to consider that others might feel differently than we do. We lived with this agreement for the better part of the school year, and it was enlightening when considered in view of the recent spate of celebrities and politicians being exposed as habitual sexual harassers and worse. These are men, and it's mostly men, who may well have been adhering to the Golden Rule as they saw it, only doing to others what they themselves would want done to them. What's missing from their actions is consent, and that's what makes it a crime.

The children's consent rule wasn't easy to enforce. Young children are forever bumping, tickling, hugging, pushing, and otherwise "doing" things to one another just in the natural flow of things. As the adult responsible for helping the children keep their agreements, I didn't feel it was my place to micromanage these sorts of day-to-day interactions, even if they did technically violate the rule of law. To do so would have meant repeatedly interrupting the children's play to remind them of their agreement to the point that there wouldn't have been much time left for the actual playing. Instead, I decided to let the kids self-manage the rule, only getting involved when a child invoked the rule of her own accord. And they did.

"Hey, you didn't ask me before you pushed me!"

"You didn't ask me if you could touch me!"

"You didn't ask me if you could sit beside me!"

"You didn't ask me if you could look at me!"

That's right, we did sometimes head down that road. Most of the time the kids invoked their rule appropriately, but we also sometimes took it too far. As the adult, it was easy to know what to do when it came to pushing. I was less confident about inadvertent touching. I had mixed feelings about children using the rule to control where people sat. And dictating where others cast their gaze was a bridge too far.

Needless to say, our consent rule created a gray area, and the only way to deal with it was through talking, sometimes lots of it, sometimes emotional. So that's what we did.

Some of the older kids began using the large dog crate on our playground as a kind of prison into which they put one another. They often played "pets." Those put into the crate were animals confined for their own "safety." The game involved lots of grabbing and wrestling, as the pets were usually feigning reluctance to being put in their cage. Watching this game as an adult was difficult. Children were "forcing" one another into a small, dark space, then barring the door with an old safety gate, holding it firmly in place while the children inside pretend to object, ultimately escaping before being chased down and returned to their prison. The game evoked so many nasty things for me, especially when it was boys forcing girls. It was a consensual game, yet the core of the game was pretending to *not* consent. Particularly upsetting for me was that the captor would often say, "I have to put you in your cage to keep you safe," while shoving another child into the hole.

As they played, I stayed nearby, waiting for that moment when I was certain they had gone too far, when someone got frightened, when it became too real and they wanted to withdraw their consent. We didn't have the consent rule on the books for this particular year, but we had agreed that if someone says "Stop!" you had to stop, which is a similar thing. A couple times I reminded kids, "Remember, if you don't like what's happening, you can say *Stop!*" but they just ignored me and continued about their game.

The truth is that none of them asked for my help, either directly or indirectly. They were playing their unsavory-looking game quite happily, managing to keep it going for long stretches despite its intensity and potential for conflict, injury, and hurt feelings. In part, they were doing it by talking and listening, the pet owners continually informing their pets about what is coming next: "I'm going to grab you and put you back in your cage," "If you get away, I'm going to catch you and bring you back," and "I can't let you get out, it's not safe." The pets in this game, as is true in real life, couldn't talk back, so their owners were forever peering into their faces, studying their expressions, looking, I think, for consent. They were forever holding on to their pets, studying their body language, *feeling*, I think, for consent. At least that's what it looked like they were doing as they played.

Over the course of a week, I gradually became more comfortable with the kids' game. Even as I continued to be bothered by the optics, I came to see that it is, at its core, a game *about* consent, about children continually checking in with one another, not with the formality of asking permission, but by "reading" one another, continually, everyone turned outward, following a rule that stands above the golden one.

How Good Ideas Get Big

A parent asked me if we could use some medical feeding bags, the kind used in hospitals for patients who can't feed themselves. I knew what she was talking about, but I had never given them much thought, let alone wanted one for the preschool.

They came in two large boxes, one of which I put on the workbench along with a couple of old tempera paint jugs full of water, and for the rest of the afternoon, we roamed the playground experimenting with them.

The kids who play at Woodland Park are already experts on water and gravity, so it wasn't long before one of them figured out that the water only ran through the hose when the nozzle was lower than the bag of water. This knowledge went viral the way knowledge does in a play-based curriculum, where the children mostly teach one another.

As I watched the play unfold, I began to think of the virality of knowledge. In this age of the Internet, we all know about videos and articles that "go viral" through the democratic process of sharing, but this, what the children were doing with the feeding bags, has always been with us. As I heard children urge one another with invitations like "Try this!" or "Look what I did!" I recognized that this is how humans have always educated themselves, with one person discovering something, then excitedly sharing it with others.

I thought of other kids who are sitting at their desks over worksheets or tests or homework. There is no virality there. In fact, we call it cheating, and you're reprimanded if you share your answers or peek over someone else's shoulder. That's one of the reasons why this sort of learning is so hard.

It's too bad because sharing is how good ideas get big.

Discovering What the Other People Are For

Both of the boys have older sisters, and one of them has a twin brother, so they have lifetimes of experience in living in a world with other children. I know they love their siblings, these people who are raising them as much as their parents are, but those have always been "arranged marriages," so to speak, people with whom they have by the circumstances of their lives been thrust. It's not the same as getting to *choose* a person the way we do when someone becomes our friend.

When I first began teaching two-year-olds, my parent educator told me, "They're all independent suns around whom the universe revolves," and while I might today be more inclined to compare this stage of their lives to one of those two star solar systems in which mother and child orbit one another, I've found the metaphor to be largely apt. At the beginning of the school year, they don't typically view the other kids as potential playmates, let alone potential friends, but over the course of the year, it begins to happen.

As I sat across the playground, I saw one of these boys take the other by the wrist. It looked to me like he was attempting to pull him along against his will. There was a moment during which they tugged against one another: one boy resistant to being pulled, and the other insistent on doing so. I began moving closer in anticipation of a conflict, but before I'd taken more than a few steps, the boy being pulled managed to calmly pry those fingers from his wrist. Words I couldn't hear were exchanged before they then took one another's hands properly, as equals, as friends, and began to walk together.

At first, they just walked about the space, neither pushing

nor pulling one another, following the contours of the playground. When one of them stepped up, he waited while the other stepped up behind him. When one stopped, the other stopped. They were accommodating one another, working together, pointing, occasionally exchanging words that I was still too far away to hear.

Eventually, they came to the bottom of a slope that we've named the Concrete Slide and opted for an ascent. They tried to do it while continuing to hold hands, but the surfaces were too steep and slippery, so they freed their hands for scrambling and one after another climbed to the top. Once up there, they exchanged more words, gesturing, then apparently agreeing to slide back down. The first one waited for the other, and they slid down side-by-side, looking into one another's faces, beaming as they did so. They agreed to do it again and again. Sometimes they agreed to take another course up or down. By now I was close enough to hear them. They were speaking sentences beginning with, "Let's..." to one another, the most magical of words.

These aren't the first butterflies to emerge from their chrysalises, nor will they be the last. I have had the privilege of witnessing this miracle of first friendships over the course of decades, but each time, it's a wonder, these first steps in the journey of discovering what the other people are really for.

A Life-Affirming Expression of Love

I've experienced it enough times to take it for granted, but whenever kids wrestle at preschool, I always at some point feel as if I'm peering into something very important, and very *good*, about human beings.

We throw down the gym mats, remind ourselves of the agreements we've made together about how to treat one another, kick off our shoes, and go. We always make common-sense agreements like to not hit or kick one another. We always agree to try to not lay hands on another person's head or neck and to only wrestle with people who have agreed to wrestle by stepping on the mats.

Since people always get hurt when we wrestle, bumped heads mostly, we have a crying chair where you can sit it out until you're ready to rejoin the fray. Some children are back from the crying chair within minutes, while others put their shoes on and walk away, judging the risks of wrestling to be a price too high.

We tend to think of wrestling as an activity that boys enjoy, and it's mostly boys who participate, but not all of them, and there are always girls who hurl their bodies into the mix.

During one session, the four- and five-year-olds wrestled with such joy, at times a dozen of them at once, grappling, rolling, dog-piling. They were laughing, making faces, and shouting, "Stop!" when things got too intense, a signal we had agreed to heed. And they did respond, as children usually do when they wrestle, almost instantly. The rule of thumb is that one must wait a minimum of fifteen seconds (often longer) for a young child to answer when asked a question or given instruction, but when they wrestle, they are so finely attuned to one another, reading expressions, listening to words, responding to how they move their bodies, anticipating, that there is minimal lag time between call and response.

When they wrestle like this, it's as if they've stopped being individuals and have joined together as a single body, each part fully conscious of and responsive to the others. They are forever checking one another's beet-red faces, reading expressions, looking there for consent, for invitations, for cautions. So often we label this sort of play as violent or aggressive, but when you really watch it, it becomes quite clear that, on the contrary, wrestling is a joyful, intense, life-affirming expression of love: a love that's so powerful that they can't keep their hands off one another.

Part Two:
Hard, Messy, Emotional Work

How We Become Wiser, Gentler People

The Secret to Making It Here, There, or Anywhere

The Story of How He Fell and Got Back Up

"They Have Never Failed to Imitate Them"

Hard, Messy, Emotional Work

Squishing Play-Dough While Discussing Urethras

That Daring Young Girl

Everything Else is Up to the Kids

Making Order from Chaos

Striving in That Direction

Why?

Where They Are the Experts

Worksheets are Always Optional

Not-So-Innocent Fun

Sacred Time

Remorse

"Bye, Bye, Butterfly!"

"I'm Going to Have This Many Babies"

The Best Stick Collector

How We Become Wiser, Gentler People

It happened in a flash. He wanted to dump the bowl of "jewels" (florist marbles) that he had collected into the mud. She wanted them to remain clean. He dumped the jewels. There were loud voices, and when I looked from across the sand pit, I saw her push his face, then storm off.

Both children were upset. The boy's mother was nearby, and after checking to make sure he wasn't hurt, engaged him in a discussion, so I followed the girl, whose body was tense with rage. She marched this way and that for a moment, jaws locked in anger. As I approached, she turned her back on me, so I stopped in my tracks.

What was I going to say to her? Maybe I was going to remind her of the rules we had all agreed to some weeks ago, specifically mentioning the "No pushing" one. I might have been preparing to say something like, "When you pushed his face, you hurt him." She walked slowly away from me, her shoulders hunched forward. When she got to a corner formed by a railing and a random cart that had found its way onto our playground, she knelt on her knees, nose in the corner.

I looked back at the boy, who was now chatting easily with his mom as he bent down to the mud, handling the jewels he had dumped there.

I didn't say anything to the girl because, frankly, there was nothing to say. Or rather, anything I said would be redundant at best. There was no question that she was already feeling remorse, regretting her action, mulling it over in the quiet of the corner she had found for herself. I stepped away and left her to her conscience. After a couple minutes, she moved herself into a more distant corner, although this time she faced outward, her face a study of sorrow, staring into the ground.

Again, I began contemplating words I might say to her. Maybe I could comment on her emotional state. Or perhaps there was something I could say to help her understand the cause and effect of the affair. But again I realized that anything I said just then would be a mere distraction from the important work she was doing, sitting alone, calming down, and painfully reflecting.

Moments later, the boy approached her, hand outstretched. In it was a jewel. He offered it to her saying, "I cleaned this one for you."

She took the jewel and held it in the palm of her hand. The boy shifted from foot to foot, as if waiting for her to say something.

When she didn't, I softly said, "That was a kind thing to do."

He went away then, back to his play. The girl watched him go, then looked back at the jewel in her hand, contemplating it for a moment before clutching it in her fist. She stayed that way, thinking and feeling, until she was ready to return to her own play. It's from these moments that we become wiser, gentler people.

The Secret to Making It Here, There, or Anywhere

Our daughter Josephine is a young adult who found her passion by the time she was an eight-year-old and who has pursued that passion to New York City, a place about which Sinatra sings, "If I can make it there, I'll make it anywhere." And from where I sit, it seems she is making it: pulling down the best grades of her life, earning money, landing internships, founding a theater company, and finding plenty of time to play with her cool friends. As I shared a story about her, someone who had never met her interrupted to ask if she had been "gifted" as a child. I think she is gifted, of course, but not in the sense that is usually meant by the term. By most measures, I'd say she has always presented as a fairly typical kid, good at some things (usually the things she enjoyed) and not so good at others (usually the things she didn't enjoy), which is more or less the way I'd describe myself.

We tried not to pressure her about school. We let her quit extracurricular activities when she wanted to quit. Finding something "boring" was more than good enough for me. With few exceptions, we didn't make her do things she didn't want to do. Of course, people warned that we were setting her up, saying things like, "How will she ever learn about perseverance?" They would caution that success only comes from putting our noses to the grindstone, while young, doing the things we don't want to do, every day as a matter of course, painting a portrait of life as relentless, competitive, and exceedingly difficult, at least if the goal was to "make it." It was easy for me to ignore them because I'd already figured out, even two decades ago, that what they were saying was pretty much pure BS, the kind of BS that is spread by tightly wound people who take life way, way, way too seriously.

There is entirely too much of this kind of BS out there, and its impact is compounded by the fact that it passes for wisdom in too many circles. Most of the time, it's just BS, but it can also be toxic, like when parents worry that their five-year-old is "falling behind," a fear that too often drives well-meaning adults to expect junior to strive to be a champion at *everything*, just in case. And that's BS.

I've never had an instinct to lead children. My driving interest is to play with them, to listen to them, to make jokes, make art, make math, make engineering, to just make things, *together*. There's no "behind" because it's about learning in the wild, about the world, about ourselves, and about what it means to be ourselves in that world. That's the fundamental question we live to answer. Everything beyond that is BS.

There was a time when I would entertain myself with the cocktail party game of asking people if there was anything their parents forced them to do that they still do today. Most people couldn't think of anything, and those that did always, *always*, cited piano lessons. Not violin lessons, not regularly attending church, not making their bed, not putting their nose to the grindstone. Indeed, it seemed that for most people, the moment their parents stopped compelling them, they ran like the wind. Yes, I'm sure that everyone can come up with exceptions to this rule, but you have to admit, it's largely true.

Putting one's nose to a grindstone is a waste of youth. Even thinking about the grindstone is an abuse. If there are grindstones in their futures, and my own life is a testament that it is not inevitable, then they will learn how to deal with them soon enough, tragically. No, if there is a *best* time for making mistakes, for chasing dreams, for indulging one's passions, for just goofing around, it's in our youth.

As I watch the children I teach play, I see them making mistakes, chasing dreams, indulging their passions, and goofing around. I don't wish wealth or fame or power or "success" on any of them. No, my hope is that they get to keep playing, throughout their lives, every day, doing those things that bring them peace and joy and love. Of course, there's crap they'll have to get through, but kids already know that. Everything they do is accompanied by pain and disappointment and conflict and fear. That's life. But when children play, when no one is harping on them about "success," but rather leaving them free to pursue their passions, it never becomes a slog. There are no grindstones. From where I sit, the only losers in life are the ones who waste it at the grindstone.

As author Kurt Vonnegut wrote, "We are here on this earth to fart around, and don't let anybody tell you different." Kids already know this. They show us that no one works harder, or perseveres more, than those who are farting around. And they also know to call BS when they see it. That is the secret to making it there or anywhere.

The Story of How He Fell and Got Back Up

As the two-year-old boy tried to walk up a short, sand-dusted concrete slope, his feet slipped from beneath him. He fell forward onto the concrete. I saw it happen. He took a moment, still prone, to look around, as if deciding if he was going to cry. When he saw me looking his way, his face wrinkled into a look of anguish, and he let it out.

I walked to him. I usually walk in circumstances like this for the same reason I strive to maintain a calm expression: running conveys panic, and the last thing I want to do is compound his pain with fear.

Taking a seat on the ground beside him, I said, "You fell." Putting a hand on his back, I said, "I came to be with you."

When he cried louder, I asked, "Did you hurt your hands?"

He shook his head. I left some silence for him to fill with the details he wanted to share, but instead he filled it with crying.

"Did you hurt your tummy?" He shook his head. "Did you hurt your chin?" This time, he nodded, still crying. I saw no mark on his chin. "It's not bleeding, but I can get you a bandage." He shook his head.

Another two-year-old boy had also seen it happen. He had joined us, looking from me to his classmate throughout the exchange.

When I left more silence, this boy decided to fill it, almost as if showing me the proper formula, bending down and asking, "Are you okay?"

This is what adults say to a fallen child, a phrase I've struck from my own lexicon, figuring that an injured child will let me know soon enough if he's hurt without my planting of the idea with that question. In this moment, however, from a two-year-old's lips, I heard it as a courtesy, like saying, "Please," "Thank you," and "How are you?"

He still cried, but not with the intensity of before, notching it down to a breathy moaning, head up, his fingers tracing paths in the dusting of sand that had been his undoing.

Yet another two-year-old boy joined us. He had not seen what had happened, and asked me, "Why is he crying?"

I replied, "He fell and hurt his chin."

"I'm a doctor."

I asked the boy who had fallen, "Do you need a doctor?"

He shook his head. There were three of us now in a circle around our friend who was winding down his cry, finishing it.

The boy who had asked "Are you okay?" took what the older kids sometimes call "the easy way" up the short slope, a path in the dirt that circumvents the slippery concrete part, intending, I thought, to go about his play. Perhaps that had been the plan, but he stopped and turned to check on his friend, saying once more, "Are you okay?"

This time, his friend nodded. His cry had become a soft whimper.

I said, "You're not crying now."

He didn't respond. His fingers fiddled with the sand until they found a twig, which he bent and twisted. I had been sitting beside him.

I said, "I'm going to get up now," which I did.

I had a vague idea that I was role modeling a possible next step for him, but he didn't immediately follow my lead. Instead, my place was taken by the doctor, who sat, as I had done, silently beside him. We're always role modeling, but we can't pick what they will chose to imitate—or even *who* will do the imitating.

I kept an eye on the situation from a few feet away. There was some conversation between the boys, but I couldn't hear it. The boy who had taken the easy way up, then climbed to the top of the slope and slid down before circling back to the scene of the fall.

By now, the boy who had fallen had completely finished his cry and was on his feet. There was more discussion amongst the three boys that I didn't hear, but judging from the body language, I'm guessing it was either about the fall or about how to best navigate the short, sand-dusted slope. Then, the two boys who had come to their friend's aid, ascended via the easy way. The boy who had fallen, however, tackled the concrete slope. His boot slipped a bit, but this time he made it without injury. He then ran back down and tried it again, then again, four times in all before he moved on.

"They Have Never Failed to Imitate Them"

Children have never been very good at listening to their elders, but they have never failed to imitate them. ~James Baldwin

I don't claim to be a parenting expert. I'm just a guy who has spent a lot of time playing with children. From that I've learned a little bit, and because of the blog I write, people approach me for my take on things. If there is any one thing that people write me more than anything else, it's something along the lines of, "I've tried everything, and nothing works." I'm talking about universal parenting aggravations like getting kids to eat their vegetables, take a nap, or participate in household chores. And these are important things. Not only do we want our children to be healthy, rested, and responsible today, but these behaviors represent the *values* of good health and responsibility that, if we can only "instill" them, we know they will serve our children throughout their lives.

While I try to be more sympathetic than this with individual readers because I know they wouldn't write to some guy on the Internet wearing a red cape unless they were truly at the end of their rope, my answer to their dilemma is really quite simple: *Quit trying.*

You can serve children healthy food, but you can't make them eat. So quit trying.

You can put children into their beds, but you can't make them sleep. So quit trying.

And you can't make them clean up their rooms without the promise of a reward or the threat of punishment. So quit trying.

Indeed, I suppose I could reply to these parents that they

haven't, in fact, tried "everything," because obviously you could always come up with a carrot that is sweet enough or a stick that is painful enough that you can *get* a child to do what you want them to do, but I would never suggest that anyone consciously step onto the vicious cycle of reward and punishment. Rewards and punishments may appear to work in the moment—the promise of ice cream may well motivate a child to eat a few peas; the threat of having toys taken away may well motivate a child to tidy up—but human nature dictates that, being unnatural consequences, the value of the rewards and the severity of the punishments must be regularly increased or they lose their effectiveness. Not only that, but the lessons taught in the long run (i.e., to be motivated by the approval or disapproval of others) are certainly not what we wish for our children. Values must come from within; they are not imposed from without. That's called obedience, an unsavory and even dangerous trait in adults.

Whatever we publicly proclaim, our actual values (as opposed to the values to which we aspire) are always, always, always most accurately and honestly revealed by our behaviors. When we eat junk food, we demonstrate that we value convenience or flavor over eating healthily. When we don't get enough sleep, we demonstrate that we value our jobs or our hobbies or our TV programs more than rest. When we let our homes become cluttered and dirty, we demonstrate that we value something else over a well-ordered household.

No, the better course, I've found, when it comes to teaching values, is to simply give up trying to make another person do something that *you* want them to do. If *you* value healthy food, then eat it. If *you* value being well rested, then sleep. If *you* value a tidy bedroom, then keep yours tidy. And ultimately, with time, sometimes lots of time, it will be your role-modeling of these behaviors that your child will come to imitate, not on your schedule, but one of his own, which is all we can expect of our fellow humans.

You cannot instill values in other people, you can only role model them. And while I've avoided mentioning them here, no matter what your priest, rabbi, pastor, imam, or guru says, this goes for moral values as well.

Hard, Messy, Emotional Work

We don't have a huge set of big wooden blocks, which is okay because we don't really have enough space for more, and besides, if the kids are going to play with them, they generally need to find a way to play with them together, which is what our school is all about.

A few years back, the most popular dramatic-play game had been "super heroes." It was mostly boys, but they weren't particularly exclusionary, with several of the girls regularly joining them, often making up their own hero names like "Super Cat" due to the lack of female characters of the type in our popular culture. This in turn inspired some of the boys to make up their own hero names like "Super Dog" and "Falcon," along with their own super powers. And although there have been a few instances of someone declaring, "We already have enough super heroes," in an attempt to close the door behind them, most of the time, the prerequisite for joining the play was to simply declare yourself a super hero, pick a super hero name, and then hang around with them, boasting about your great might, creating hideouts, and bickering over nuance.

Before long, however, a breakaway group began playing, alternatively, *Paw Patrol* and *Pokémon*, which looked to me like essentially the same game with new characters. One day, some boys playing *Paw Patrol* used all of the big wooden blocks to create their "house," complete with beds and blankets. A girl who was often right in the middle of the superhero play wanted to join them, but when they asked, "Who are you?" she objected to being a *Paw Patrol* character at all. Indeed, she wanted to play with them and with the blocks they were using, but the rub was that she didn't want to play their game.

After some back and forth, during which the *Paw Patrol* kids tried to find a way for her to be included, they offered her a few of their blocks to play with on her own, then went back to the game.

She arranged her blocks, then sat on them, glaring at the boys. They ignored her. I was sitting nearby watching as her face slowly dissolved from one of anger to tears. An adult tried to console her, but was more or less told to back off.

I waited a few minutes, then sat on the floor beside her, saying, "You're crying."

She answered, "I need more blocks." I nodded. She added, "They have all the blocks."

I replied, "They are using most of the blocks, and you have a few of the blocks."

"They won't give me any more blocks."

I asked, "Have you asked them for more blocks?"

Wiping at her tears, she shook her head. "No."

"Maybe they don't know you want more blocks."

She called out, "Can I have some more blocks?"

The boys stopped playing briefly, one of them saying, "We're using them!"

Then another added, "You can have them when we're done," which is our classroom mantra around "sharing."

She went back to crying, looking at me as if to say, *See?*

I said, "They said you can use them when they're done... Earlier I heard them say you could play *Paw Patrol* with them."

"I don't want to play *Paw Patrol*. I just want to build."

I sat with her as the boys leapt and laughed and lurched. I pointed out that there was a small building set that wasn't being used in another part of the room, but she rejected that, saying, "I want to build with *these* blocks."

I nodded, saying, "I guess we'll just have to wait until they're done." That made her cry some more.

This is hard stuff we're working on here in preschool. And, for the most part, that's pretty much all we do at Woodland Park: figuring out how to get along with the other people. Most days aren't so hard, but there are moments in every day when things don't go the way we want or expect them to, and then, on top of getting along with the other people, there are our own emotions with which we must deal. Academic types call it something like "social-emotional functioning," but I think of it as the work of creating a community.

It's a tragedy that policymakers are pushing more and more "academics" into the early years, because it's getting in the way of this very real, very important work the children need to do if they are going to lead satisfying, successful lives. In our ignorant fearfulness about Johnny "falling behind," we are increasingly neglecting what the research tells us about early learning.

According to a CNN story about a study conducted by researchers from Penn State and Duke Universities:

> Teachers evaluated the kids based on factors such as whether they listened to others, shared materials, resolved problems with their peers and were helpful. Each student was then given an overall score to rate their positive skills and behavior, with zero representing the lowest level and four for students who demonstrated the

highest level of social skill and behavior...Researchers then analyzed what happened to the children in young adulthood, taking a look at whether they completed high school and college and held a full-time job, and whether they had any criminal justice, substance abuse or mental problems...For every one-point increase in a child's social competency score in kindergarten, they were twice as likely to obtain a college degree and 46% more likely to have a full-time job by age 25...For every one-point decrease in a child's social skill score in kindergarten, he or she had a 67% higher chance of having been arrested in early adulthood, a 52% higher rate of binge drinking and an 82% higher chance of being in or on a waiting list for public housing.

This is far from the only research that has produced these and similar results.

If our goal is well-adjusted, "successful" citizens, we know what we need to do. In the early years, it isn't about reading or math. It's not about learning to sit in desks or filling out worksheets or queuing up for this or that. If we are really committed to our children, we will recognize that their futures are not dependent upon any of that stuff, but rather this really hard, messy, emotional work we do every day as we play with our fellow citizens.

Squishing Play-Dough While Discussing Urethras

We were gathered together around a fresh ball of play-dough, five girls and Teacher Tom.

"Teacher Tom, look at my butt!"

"I don't want to look at your butt." I said it in such a way that they took it as a joke.

"Teacher Tom, look at *my* butt!"

"I don't want to look at anyone's butt."

"If I pulled down my pants and underpants, you would see my butt."

"I don't want you to do that. I'm perfectly fine *not* seeing your butt."

There was some general giggling, then, "Why don't you want to see my butt?"

"I guess it's because that's where your poop comes out, and I'm not a big fan of poop."

The word made them giggle some more. Then one of the girls added, "And it's where pee comes out, too!"

This assertion brought the frivolity to a pause as everyone let it sink in. Then one of them objected. "Pee doesn't come out of your butt."

"It does. I feel it sometimes."

"It doesn't. I think that's called diarrhea. Pee comes out of your vulva."

"You mean vagina."

"No, I don't. My vagina is the inside part you can't see. My vulva is the outside."

There was a general looking around at one another as if for confirmation. Then someone said, "I don't think that's right. Pee doesn't come from the outside part, it comes from the inside. There's another hole it comes out of..."

"Is it the labia?"
"No... I know! It's the urethra."
"That's right, the pee comes out of the urethra. That's what my body book says."

No one looked to me for either confirmation or information, because they obviously didn't need it.

That Daring Young Girl

When the children don't need me, which is most of the time, I sometimes unobtrusively putter about the classroom. I'll pick puzzle pieces or play-dough off the floor or right an overturned chair, but only once I'm sure the things are genuinely discarded and not actually "in use." Often I will find popular items abandoned in out-of-the-way places and I return them to their expected places so that the children who are looking for them will know where to find them.

One day, I discovered that one of our two-year-olds had dumped the tray of plastic cutlery into the basin of our pretend kitchen sink. These are daily-use items, and while they hadn't travelled far from their usual place, I figured I'd return them to where they live.

Usually, the children ignore me as I tidy up, but in this case, one girl took an interest.

"What are you doing?" she asked so softly that I almost couldn't hear her.

"I'm just putting the forks and knives and spoons back into the tray."

Without a word, she began to help me. In fact, I just stepped back as she shouldered the responsibility as her own. One-by-one, she carefully placed the individual pieces of cutlery side by side in the tray, taking care that I'd not have taken to make sure they were all facing the same direction. Indeed, I don't know her system, but she seemed to hesitate before placing each piece, deciding purposefully among the three sections of the tray. When she was done, she picked up the tray and put it on the shelf where it belongs. She didn't turn to me for approval or even acknowledge me in any way as she then went about her business.

Later, on the playground, I was talking with an adult visitor to our school. We were standing near the swings where several children played. Few of these young children had figured out how to "pump," so they were mostly just hanging there, kicking at the ground to create a little momentum. I mentioned to the guest that our general policy is that adults don't push kids on the swings. As we observed, one girl approached another who was sitting on our tire swing. She stood looking for a moment, regarding her classmate just hanging there, sizing up the situation, then, without a word, took her position and began to push the swing in a gentle back-and-forth arc. It was the same sort of wordless shouldering of responsibility that I'd experienced earlier with the cutlery.

The more I've learned to stay out of the children's play, the more I trust not just their competence, but their ability to unselfishly regard the other people and to seek to help them. I'm reminded of Jon Muth's picture book *The Three Questions*, which is based upon a short story of the same name by Leo Tolstoy. From the conclusion of Tolstoy's philosophical story about a king seeking truth:

> Remember then: there is only one time that is important—Now! It is the most important time because it is the only time when we have any power. The most necessary man is he with whom you are...and the most important affair is to do him good, because for that purpose alone was man sent into this life!

It's a truth that I feel in my own heart, even if I often struggle to live it, but the more time I've spent with young children, the more I stay out of their way, the more I see that they are the ones who truly understand it, not intellectually, of course, but by simply living in the "Now," regarding their fellow humans in their toils or trials and making a decision to help them. This is why I can never consider adults as more intelligent than children. This is why I do not see "development" as a one-way street. There are things we learn as we gain experience, but I know that we simultaneously lose an equal amount wisdom, wisdom that would serve us all if only we could find a way to not un-learn it.

Everything Else is Up to the Kids

I get a lot of credit for things I didn't do. Grateful parents are forever thanking me for "teaching" their children things that they would have learned with or without me, or our preschool, or any school at all for that matter. I accept the thanks or reflect it back to them, crediting them as "great parents," but the truth is that most of what their children have learned they would have learned with nothing more or less than a community, our love, and the freedom to pursue their own interests.

Children hate school because they love freedom. ~Peter Gray

One of the things I get the most credit for is helping children learn to "love learning," another compliment that I can only accept with a certain amount of guilt because all humans are born with that love for learning. Indeed, that's what play is: the instinct to educate oneself made manifest. Play is what children do to make sense of their world. In everything they freely do, we see children asking and answering their own questions, educating themselves. I often think that my real accomplishment is that children spend three years attending the Woodland Park Cooperative School without learning to hate school, which is something about which I have mixed feelings, because I can't help but think it's a bit of a set up: as long as they go on to attend normal schools, the "hate" is coming, because the freedom to pursue their own interests is going to be slowly throttled. I make myself feel better by convincing myself that we are fattening them up in order to better survive the famines ahead.

Oh sure, they may still, on balance, enjoy school, and there will be parts they enjoy very much, but from where I sit, that's more a testament to the resiliency of children than anything else. One of the happiest parts of being a teacher is seeing my former students all grown up; one of the saddest parts is when they tell me they're excited for a long weekend because they "don't have to go to school." When they attended Woodland Park, they cried when they learned that school was closed over the holidays. So, while hate may be too strong a word, they all certainly come to have mixed feelings, and for some it grows into the idea that they hate learning altogether.

Some will assert that this is the natural order of things, that they must learn to take the good with the bad, to endure, to have "grit," to persevere through their hate. Indeed, there are those who believe that our kind of school does children a disservice by not doing more to get the children "school ready," which seems to mean teaching them to hate school at least a little bit before they get to elementary school, where the hate is inevitable. I will not do that to children. If they must come to hate learning, even a little, I'll leave that to the fun-stealers in their futures.

Learning can only happen when a child is interested. If he is not interested, it's like throwing marshmallows at his head and calling it eating. ~Katrina Gutleben

Some will assert that the fault lies with the teachers, that they aren't being creative enough, that they haven't employed all the tricks to "make learning fun," that if we would just "gamify" it, or something, then the kids would be happy learners. The problem with this is that children are already happy learners—they were born that way—but they were also born to learn through their own interests, not the compulsion of others. Forcing children to "learn" things that hold no interest is like forcing a person to eat when they aren't hungry or to sleep when they aren't tired: you can do it, but it will always be a battle for everyone involved.

If children started school at six months old and their teachers gave them walking lessons, within a single generation people would come to believe that humans couldn't learn to walk without going to school. ~Geoff Graham

And therein lies the crux of the problem: normal schools attempt to replace a child's natural interests with a curriculum full of crap that kids couldn't care less about. On top of that is the hubris that these children will learn nothing without adults standing over them "teaching" every step of the way. If children started school at six months, teachers like me would even be congratulated for their learning to talk and walk. This is what has happened with so many of the things we try to "teach" in normal schools, like reading and basic math. Humans taught themselves to learn these useful, necessary things for hundreds and thousands of years, at their own pace, through their own interests, before they were made compulsory through schooling. (For those who doubt this, I must reiterate that literacy rates in America were higher 250 years ago than they are today, well before widespread compulsory schooling.)

Sometimes a parent will thank me for something for which I really do feel responsible. They will thank me for helping to create the Woodland Park "community," a place in which their child has thrived. I accept those compliments without an ounce of doubt because, after all, that is the main role of adults when it comes to the education of children: to create a real community full of connection, cooperation, and love. When we do that, we do all we must. Everything else is up to the kids.

Making Order from Chaos

We were playing with our Mah Jong tiles. We don't play the actual game because I don't think any of us know how, but I trot them out every now and then because they come in a nice little case, and the smooth, heavy game pieces are a pleasure to handle. There are always a few kids who take an interest in them, often building small table-top structures, but they are even more often left alone for long stretches of our days together. At one point, I passed the unoccupied table where I'd put them to start the day to find that one of the kids had arranged them purposefully. I hadn't seen who had done it, but he or she had apparently been studying the markings and had played a quiet matching game.

I love these sorts of discoveries, evidence of a child's brain at work. I find several each day, but the story they tell is not always this clear, so I took a few photos. Later, at the end of the day, I found that someone had put them all into his or her carrying case, failing to arrange them with the care it takes to make them fit properly. The lid was nevertheless snapped shut, albeit warped from the disorder within. I have no way of knowing if this was the work of the same child or not, but whoever it was had struggled to get that lid to close, as evidenced by the way it bulged over the improperly stacked tiles.

Not long thereafter, we were celebrating Valentine's Day. We have several empty bulk candy cans that we use as playthings. I had positioned several Valentine's Day themed items on our red table and thought the cans were suitably festive enough to include there as well. I had a vague idea the kids would enjoy putting things into those cans, and they did, stuffing them full, dumping them out, carrying them by their handles.

At the end of the day, I found that the cans had been returned to the table, but the rest of the Valentine's materials were missing. I hunted in the most likely places, but no luck. I even went down the hall to check the kids' cubbies, thinking that perhaps someone had attempted to take the prized items home—it happens. Finally, feeling a bit frustrated, I opened the cans and, sure enough, that's where the materials had been stashed. I should have known, but as I opened each can, removing the contents in preparation for the following day, I realized that this stuff had not been tucked away randomly: there was one can for the love rats, one for the love ducks, one for the heart puzzles, and so on. I was immediately reminded of my mysterious Mah Jong arranger.

Not long after that, I'd placed our four "Barrel of Monkeys" sets on that same red table. At the end of the day, I found that someone had taken the time to sort the red ones into the red barrel, the green into the green barrel, and the blue ones into the two blue barrels. This was starting to become a mystery I needed to solve.

A few days later as I was going through some photos, I'd snapped. I saw that someone had meticulously sorted our large collection of buttons by color. So the following day, I planted myself at the button table, determined to figure out who it was. I sat there a long time, but finally, as I was about to give up my vigil, my mystery organizer revealed himself by quietly recreating the photos I'd taken the day before.

I watched him go about his business, admiring his concentration, and experiencing his satisfaction of making order from chaos by proxy. Mystery solved.

Striving in That Direction

A common characteristic of play-based schools are policies discouraging adults from helping children with things they can do for themselves. This goes for everyday personal care things like putting on jackets and using the toilet, as well as physical challenges like climbing to the top of the playhouse or using the swings.

Ideally, we step back as they engage their struggles. When they begin to get frustrated, we might support them with narrative statements like, "You've put your arm in the sleeve" or perhaps helpful informative statements like, "Your other sleeve is behind you." When it's something necessary like dressing appropriately for outdoors or peeing in the potty, we then might step in with actual assistance when it appears the challenge is still too much for them, but only after giving each child a chance to do what he can for himself. When it's something with which the child is challenging herself, like climbing a tree, we might move closer and offer words of encouragement, or say things like, "I won't help you, but I won't let you get hurt."

Competence is built upon perseverance, and these struggles with meaningful, real-world challenges (as opposed to the manufactured challenges of tests and homework) are the foundations upon which confident, self-motivated humans are built.

As a cooperative preschool in which parents work in the classroom as assistant teachers, this is one of the most important and difficult lessons some parents learn. Teachers who have never worked in a cooperative often ask me if parents "get in the way" or intervene too much or too quickly, and my answer is, "Yes, they do." When families arrive at our school with their two-year-olds, many are still brand new to the parenting game, primarily experienced in caring for infants who need so much done for them. For first time parents, that is the only parent-child relationship they know, and while there was a time when it frustrated me, I've come to realize that part of my job is to recognize where they are on their journey and to be there as they, and their child, transition into this new phase.

In other words, we don't always live up to our ideal, but rather, as is the case with any ideal, we always strive in that direction.

The "unicycle merry-go-round" is one of the features of our outdoor classroom. It's made to sit on a paved surface, which we had when we acquired it, but it's now installed on sloped, wood-chip-covered ground. There's a "track" upon which the wheels are meant to turn, but it's almost always blocked with wood chips and other debris making it nearly impossible for children to peddle. At the beginning of the school year, in our 2's class in particular, there is almost always an adult bent to the task of pushing the children.

But as time passes, I know that this is one of the places where I'll see clear evidence of the progress we've made along our journey. The adults will begin to stand back without my encouragement as their children struggle with the apparatus. We will wait as the kids identify the wood-chips-on-the-track problem themselves. They will find brooms to sweep the track. Some will choose to be "riders" while others will be "motors," pushing one another around and around, taking turns by an unspoken system of their own devising, while the adults stand back, not helping, all of us striving toward our ideal.

Why?

My mother-in-law was unenthusiastic about her restaurant dessert. "It's chocolate, whipped cream, and hazelnuts. In my generation, people would have just said, 'Why?'" There was a pause around the dinner table, then we all burst into laughter.

"Why?" indeed.

It's a good question. It's always a good question, one that young preschoolers are famous for asking, often annoyingly so. My own daughter Josephine hit the "Why?" phase during her three-year-old year. I chose to not let it get under my skin and instead attempted, in the spirit of a game, to honestly answer the question whenever and wherever we were, going deeper and deeper and deeper until we came to the place where my only honest answer was, "I don't know, but we can find out." It's the game played by scientists and philosophers, theologians and toddlers, one that is infinitely deep, each answer spawning another "Why?"

I understand why overwhelmed adults might find such a seemingly endless game aggravating, but it's important to know that they aren't doing it to get on your nerves. Most of the time, it's a genuine attempt to get closer to the truth, as each answer leads to more questions, much the way that there is always one more shovelful of sand to remove from a hole. Sometimes the questions lead back to themselves, creating an endless loop. Sometimes they lead to a parsing of parsings. Sometimes they open up the universe.

One day, Josephine met another slightly younger girl amongst the toys at Ikea who turned the tables on her, asking "Why?" to every one of her answers. Finally, in frustration, Josephine said, "Stop asking that question!" And from that moment forward, the "Why?" phase was done at our house. I suppose it's the repetition that gets under our skins, as it did with Josephine, but I often wonder if it goes deeper than that. If we don't just answer perfunctorily, the chain of "Why?" takes us, step by step, towards an "I don't know" that we can't "find out," a place where speculation is all we have. We are left with the unknown, an uncomfortable place to be for many of us.

We all know where "Why?" ultimately leads us, even if it enlightens us until it doesn't. That's why we paused before we laughed at my mother-in-law's dessert critique: we needed a moment to let our minds follow the logic of her question. But then we laughed from our bellies because the alternative is to cry all day.

At some point, we learn to stop asking "Why?" if only because we don't want to irritate the other people, but I hope that when we stop asking it aloud we continue to at least ask it of ourselves and to let the answers, or at least the pursuit of those answers, continue to guide us into the places where "Why?" cannot be answered.

Where They Are the Experts

"Loose parts" is something of a trendy concept among us progressive early childhood educators, although I prefer to call it "junk and debris" because it is a self-defining term. Research consistently finds that children engaged in loose-parts play use more math language and more elaborate vocabulary than children playing with traditional toys or during structured play. But why is that?

No one knows for sure, of course, but I expect that it has to do with the fact that open-ended, unscripted playthings cause children to engage in more cooperative play, which requires communication, not with adults, but with other kids who are likewise learning math and vocabulary. Whereas "toys" and adult-led activities tend to be more predictable, with many of their answers built into them, children interacting with loose parts are more likely to run across new concepts and unexpected challenges, situations that require children to stretch themselves in order to communicate with one another.

For instance, children building with familiar unit blocks, with their regular sizes and flat edges, are playing in a relatively predictable environment, one that is less likely to present new concepts or unexpected challenges. Children building with a collection of pinecones, sticks, rocks, and leaves, on the other hand, are playing with far less standardized building materials, ones that take children to places where they must find new language to communicate about things like relative density, shape, size, fragility, texture, and other aspects of their materials. The answers are not built into these materials.

Whenever children play together without the interference of adults, they are creating their own world, not just through their physical project, but also through the words and concepts they discover and communicate about together. Often the words they use are imprecise at first, leading to disagreements and confusion. Often they misinterpret concepts, leading to faulty theories. As they continue to play, however, as they learn more about the world they are creating, their language tends to become more precise and their theories more refined. I enjoy few things more than when children begin using terminology of their own devising, their own shortcut jargon, to describe phenomena they have discovered together.

This is why giving children the chance to engage in unstructured play with junk and debris is so powerful; it removes most of the "scripts" that are baked into regular toys and structured play, freeing children to create a world of their own, a place where they are the experts.

Worksheets are Always Optional

My heart goes out to all those preschoolers who are today and every day being compelled to do stuff, not because it's stuff they need to do, not because it's the good or right thing to do, and certainly not because it's the best thing to do, but because someday down the road, the reasoning goes, other adults are going to seek to compel them to do things they would rather not do, and so we might as well get them used to it.

Frankly, I hope they never get used to it. A few years ago, one of my former students moved on to a public school kindergarten, where he refused to do his worksheets. While the other kids bent over them, he goofed around. After a couple weeks, the teacher, at her wit's end, sent the entire stack of worksheets home with the boy, expecting his mother to march him through them. Both parent and child refused. As I said to the mother at the time, "What are they going to do, expel him? What are they going to do, give him an F in worksheets? And even if they did, what difference will it make in his life?"

Most of the children I teach manage "just fine" (a melancholy measurement, if you ask me) when confronted by the compulsory nature of normal schools. They might not like it, but they resign their noses to the grindstone after a while, and I take pride in at least not being the one who bent them to it. And it's true that many of the kids I teach go on to thrive in public schools despite having spent the previous several years not being compelled in preparation for being compelled, which kind of puts the lie to the arguments of the "school readiness" crowd.

Our playground is built on a slope, making it inevitable that children will regularly get the idea to roll things down it. Among the things they like to roll are old car tires. They wrestle them to the top of the short flight of stairs that descend from the gate, wrestle them onto the ramp they make from a plank of wood, then call out their cautions before letting them go. Other kids, seeking to keep themselves and others safe, create a wall of junk halfway down the hill near the garden, continually repairing it as the tires crash into it. Other children mill about in between, thrilling themselves by standing in the way of the tires, then leaping aside at the last second. At any given moment, there will be anywhere from five to a dozen of them engaged in the game in some way, creating, experimenting, cooperating, playing. No one is telling them what to do. Instead, they are doing what they were born to do, asking and answering their own questions about their world and the people they find there.

These children are preparing themselves for life much more directly and effectively than those bent over desks filling out worksheets from which they may or may not be learning anything, but certainly not what they most need or want to learn. Instead, they spend their days practicing for the decades of compulsory schooling ahead, rather than life itself, a place where worksheets are always optional.

Not-So-Innocent Fun

I was being a tourist, sauntering along Laugavegur, the main shopping street of downtown Reykjavík, Iceland. As I paused in front of a shop window, I noticed a pair of boys I judged to be around eight years old. They stood out to me first and foremost because they were apparently unescorted by an adult, a sight I rarely see in the US, even in smaller towns, and while Reykjavík isn't a huge city, it's still a place full of traffic and strangers and other urban "dangers."

I was also struck by the fact that they were being sneaky, keeping to a wall, knees bent, up on their toes as if trying to stay quietly out of sight, perhaps creeping up on someone they planned to startle. They were alive and alert, focused, not paying any mind to the American tourist who was watching them. As they came out into the open, they slowed and crouched even more. Then with a quick synchronized motion, they tossed what looked to be small pebbles through the doorway of a shop entrance that stood open at the top of a short flight a stairs. Then they ran. They bolted toward an alleyway, scrambled over a high fence, and they were gone, probably giggling together with red-faced excitement. I waited for someone to emerge from the shop to scold them, but apparently their naughtiness was noticed only by me.

These were not the only unsupervised children I saw in Reykjavík. Indeed, it's quite common to spy groups of girls and boys out and about in the world, a sight that takes me back to my own childhood. Most of them were not attempting to get into trouble, of course, but that's definitely always a possibility when there are no stern grown-ups around to stop them with their scolding. That's always one of the possibilities of freedom.

I've been there myself: running away, leaping fences, ducking around corners, hiding, giggling in the face of the danger of escape. Without going into my own particular offenses, I can tell you that I would not be who I am today without those moments of "crime" committed simply for the thrill of avoiding punishment. And I didn't always avoid punishment of either the natural or unnatural variety.

It's in the nature of childhood to experiment with danger, be it heights or speed or being lost. We are designed to test our boundaries, including social ones, and that requires being out from under the watchful eye of adults.

I felt a thrill at witnessing these impish boys having their not-so-innocent fun. It carried me back to those vital times that I recall with the sharp clarity that accompanies having done something that affected you deeply. I lament that American children are missing out on this type of danger play, even as I know they are still doing it whenever and wherever they find a crack in parental surveillance. And even if a parent somehow manages to keep their child under lock and key, I know that when the day finally comes that they are free, they will play catch up, often in ways far more dangerous than tossing stones through shop doorways.

Sacred Time

Ninety percent of our days at Woodland Park are spent in "unstructured" play, which is to say that the children are responsible for choosing what they are going to do and how they are going to do it. They make their own decisions, set their own goals, negotiate and collaborate with the other people, and learn how their own behaviors and emotions, and those of others, impact upon their results. When children are engaged in "structured" activities, adults are responsible for choosing what they are going to do and how they are going to do it. Adults make the decisions, set the goals, dictate rules, and determine acceptable behaviors and even emotions.

Most schools are not like Woodland Park. Most children spend their school days engaged in structured activities, moving from this pre-determined thing to the next. I attended a "play-based kindergarten" as a boy (or what we used to just call "kindergarten"). When I hit first grade, however, the structure set in. I was good at school, even enjoying most of it, but we all lived for recess, the one time of the day where no one was telling us what to do. Indeed, we did what we could to avoid inviting adult intervention, settling our own disputes, managing our own behaviors and emotions because we all intuitively knew that once an adult was involved, our fun was at stake. The boys would organize themselves into huge kickball games, complete with negotiated rules that were self-enforced. There were adults around, in the distance, supervising, but even if one was injured, our ethic was to avoid involving them unless there was a lot of blood.

At the end of the day, we went home without homework

to our lives of unstructured play. Today, that isn't the case for far too many children, who are instead shuttled off to music lessons, sports teams, and other "enrichment" programs after school and on weekends, structured activities intended to make them smarter or more well-rounded or perhaps just to occupy them while parents finish their work days. But at what cost?

According to a study conducted by psychologists at the universities of Colorado and Denver, "Structured time could slow the development of self-control":

> When children spend more time in structured activities, they get worse at working toward goals, making decisions, and regulating their behavior... Instead, kids might learn more when they have the responsibility to decide for themselves what they're going to do with their time...they found that the kids who spent more time in less-structured activities had more highly-developed self-directed executive function.

Traditional schools have always been places that are largely dominated by structured activities. What has changed since I was a boy is that so many of our children spend their non-school hours bent over homework or participating in adult-directed environments, following instructions rather than thinking for themselves. Executive function, that part of our mental process that allows us to work productively toward achieving goals and manage our behaviors and emotions, is largely developed in childhood and the surest way to develop that is through practice, yet too many kids get precious little of it. If we want our children to grow into self-directed and competent adults, then we must set them free to play.

As children, we considered Saturdays and that time between the end of school and bedtime as sacred, our time, resenting every imposition on it. We played in our garages and backyards, in the street and in our bedrooms, with others and alone, practicing being self-directed humans, which is ultimately every parent's goal. The only way we'll get there is to help our children take back that sacred time.

Remorse

The four- and five-year-olds were working hard at the beginning of the school year, striving to figure out who we were going to be as a community. Our list of agreements with our self-created rules was already quite long. We had agreed, for instance, to not hit one another and to not snatch things from other people, essentials, I think, for any society in which I would choose to live.

There had been a lot of legislation about throwing things. Indeed, we had already banned the throwing of wood chips, sand, rocks, sticks, toys, and "anything that's hard." We had specified, in particular, that these things not be thrown at faces, heads, or eyes. Some of these agreements came straight out of experience, but most derived, thankfully, from extrapolation or mental experiments.

We were also learning that agreeing to rules doesn't necessarily mean everyone will always abide by them. We coach the children to stand up for themselves, to say, "Stop!" when someone is harming or frightening them, and it comes naturally for some kids, while others either forget in the heat of the moment or feel intimidated. These children will have plenty of opportunities to practice, however, as we steer our way through a long school year. The ultimate goal, one that we will always be working toward, but never fully attain, is a truly self-governing community, one in which the children know to remind one another about their agreements. We usually come closer to that ideal than many adult communities, but they still need, or at least think they need, quite a bit of adult support when conflict arises.

One day, at least a dozen kids approached me at different times to report rule violations by this or that child. Most of the time, especially when they didn't appear particularly emotional, I simply sent them back into the fray with my best advice, which most of the time is to say to their friends, "You pushed me. I didn't like that," or "You threw sand in my hair! Stop it!"

One boy, in particular, was having a tough time of it. At least a half dozen kids reported minor rule violations on his part within a matter of minutes, so I had a one-on-one chat with him, reminding him of the agreements he had made, telling him what the other children had said to me, asking if there was anything I could do to help him remember his agreements. He seemed concerned and contrite.

Later in the day, he threw an old watering can and it hit the ground with such force that it broke into pieces. It was one of those moments when everything around him grew silent.

I stepped in, saying as matter-of-factly as I could, "You broke the watering can."

His face was ashen. He said, "I forgot," and without prompting, he began to pick up the pieces, collecting them on his lap.

I then said more than I should have. "We all agreed, no throwing hard things. You threw a hard thing and it broke."

He said, "I'll fix it," to which I replied, "We can't fix broken plastic, but you can throw it away."

"I will."

As he gathered the rest of the pieces, I could tell he was fighting down tears. I helped him gather the remaining bits, saying things like, "You didn't mean to break it." As he ran down the hill toward the garbage can, he began to cry, hard, tears of genuine and painful remorse. He felt awful, and I did too. Despite my efforts, my tone had been harsher than I would have liked, my words too many. He ran into the play-house and threw himself into a corner, bawling. I followed him, saying, "It's all right," but he didn't want me there.

"Go away!" he cried.

I asked another adult to sit with him in case he needed someone. It was near the end of the day, so the rest of us went inside to read our story while he remained outside with his remorse. He was not alone, but I expect he felt that way. The parent who sat with him said that he had spoken aloud to himself, processing what had happened, bemoaning the broken watering can and other things.

I could have handled it better. I went home feeling my own remorse, and I would return the next day committed to doing better. I expect that was true for him as well.

"Bye, Bye, Butterfly!"

For several years, the grandfather of two of the children enrolled in our school took it upon himself to purchase caterpillars, ladybug larva, and praying mantis egg sacs for the school. It was the gift of metamorphosis, a process that we watched over the course of a few weeks. For whatever reason, our classroom climate must have been perfect one year, because every single caterpillar pupated quickly and became a fully formed painted lady butterfly. In years past, there had always been one or two that didn't make it or that emerged from their chrysalises somehow deformed and unable to fend, but those, to my eye, were as nature intended.

I had been telling the children the "story" of the butterfly lifecycle over and over again. Each time children gathered around to peer at the caterpillars or chrysalises, I would say, "Caterpillars are born from tiny eggs, and they eat leaves and get bigger, then they split their skins and form their chrysalises where they turn into butterflies. After they emerge, we will let them go outside so they can find mates and lay eggs so we will have more caterpillars."

Sometimes they ask me to tell it again and again, especially the youngest children. We have a song we sing about the process. We compare this story to that of the ladybugs or to the seeds we've planted. I usually call them "circle stories" because they go on and on, round and round. Some of the older children have started identifying other circle stories, like the ones about weeks or seasons or even our own human lifecycle.

The lifetime of a butterfly is short, only a couple weeks. In years past, we had made the mistake of keeping them in their cages too long, releasing them when they're already too geriatric to fulfill their part in the lifecycle, except as food for something else. That's why this time I made sure to emphasize the part about us letting them go outside. I wanted the children to know it was coming.

When the time came, we took the butterflies outside. They had been quite active indoors in their cage, but outside where it was a bit breezy, they grew still, something the children noticed.

"Maybe they're shy."

"I think they're scared."

"I don't think they want to leave us."

Then finally, one fluttered out and away into the sky. Spontaneously, all of us, the children and their parents, called out, "Bye, bye, butterfly!" As we stood waiting for the next to take flight, one of the girls urged everyone to take a step back so the butterflies could feel "safer." Her classmates complied. Then another took to the sky to a chorus of "Bye, bye, butterfly!" One by one over the course of the next fifteen minutes, they launched themselves. A couple failed, tumbling to the ground, a dangerous place on a playground, but we were careful, waiting with still feet until they finally figured it out. The last one was reluctant to leave. It was still feeding on the sugar water we had manufactured to feed them, but finally it too fluttered away as we called after it, "Bye, bye, butterfly."

When the last one was gone, a boy burst into tears. He had wanted to keep one. I told him the story again, the circle story about butterflies, about us all, but it didn't console him, at least not right away. One of the butterflies then made another pass overhead, hunting for food, looking for a mate. I pointed it out to the boy, who stopped crying long enough to notice it.

He said, his eyes still awash, "Bye, bye, butterfly."
And then it was gone, off to fulfill its destiny.

The Butterfly upon the Sky,
That doesn't know its Name
And hasn't any tax to pay
And hasn't any Home
Is just as high as you and I,
And higher, I believe,
So soar away and never sigh
And that's the way to grieve—
~Emily Dickinson

"I'm Going to Have This Many Babies"

"I'm going to have this many babies." She held up all ten fingers.

I replied, "That's a lot of babies."

"Yes, I'm going to have five girl babies and five boy babies."

"You're going to have to come up with a lot of names for that many babies."

"No, actually I won't because I'm going to name all the girl babies…" She paused to think. "Calla! And I'm going to name all the boy babies…Darla!"

"That will be convenient," I said. "If you want to call all the girls, you can just say, *Callas!*"

We were sitting on the ground outdoors. There were a couple other kids within earshot. A boy named Arthur chimed in, "I think you should name all the boys Arthur."

"Okay, I'll name all the boys Arthur."

A boy with a sister named Cecelia suggested, "I think you should name all the girls Cecelia."

"Okay, the girls will be named Cecelia, but their nicknames will be Nina. And the boys' nicknames will be Arjun."

I nodded. "That sounds complicated."

"Not for me."

"No, I imagine not. You're the mom."

"That's right, but you know I'm going to have to find a dad. You need a dad to make a baby. I think I'll pick Sebi." Sebi was the name of a boy who was passing by us at the moment.

Hearing his name, he stopped. "What?"

"I need you to be the dad of my babies, okay?"

"Sure."

"You'll just have to give me some sperm so I can hatch the eggs."

"Sure," he answered again before racing off.

She seemed satisfied. "I'm not going to have my babies when I'm a kid. I'm going to wait until I'm older, maybe one hundred."

"Fair enough," I answered.

"And you can be the grandpa... If you're not dead."

The Best Stick Collector

"I'm the best stick collector." He had said it to me earnestly, as if telling me something I didn't already know. His cubby, the place designated for his personal belongings, was always overflowing with sticks. His mother told me that he had a similar collection at home near their front porch. As he boasted of his stick collecting expertise, he was wielding a length of bamboo. When I remarked on it, he informed me that one of his friends had found an identical one, but he had lost it, while he, the great stick collector, still had his.

He brought sticks from home. He found sticks on the way to school. He found them on the playground. The world was covered in sticks, and he, the best stick collector, had an eye for those worthy of his collection.

At any given moment, he had a stick in his hand, an extension of his body, a fantasy ninja weapon, a tool, a pointer, an instrument of science. He waved his sticks around, flourishing them in sudden bursts according to the script that was always playing in his head. Sometimes adults who weren't aware that he was the best stick collector would warn him to be careful not to poke or hit his classmates, but I never worried about him. He seemed to always be aware of his body in space, including those sticks, which were mere extensions of it.

The best stick collector focused on relatively short sticks, typically not longer than twelve inches, leaving the longer ones to the amateurs. He favored ridged sticks because, it seemed, he preferred precision tools. Upon occasion, I discovered sticks that I thought he might like, offering them to him the way one might an unusual stamp to a philatelist.

Most often, he rejected them with only a glance, but every now and then, he would take a closer look, studying it for a time. Once, and only once, he accepted my find as worthy, although it wound up in his cubby with the back-ups, never entering the rotation of favored sticks.

He was a connoisseur, a prodigy, a master. He was the best stick collector, and he was my friend.

Part Three:
What It Means to Be Equal and Free

A Good STEM Education is a Play-Based One

"But How Do They Learn to Read?"

Don't Buy the "Falling Behind" Snake Oil

The Evidence Tells Us We Should Set Kids Free

"Teach by Doing Whenever You Can"

Too Many "Tripping Hazards"

As If Mathematics Was Coded into Our Genes

How a Junkyard Playground Works

"Play with a Purpose"

My Adult Sense of Justice

"It's Not a Drum"

How I Would Start to Transform Public Education

Meetings

Transitions

What It Means to Be Equal and Free

Rabble Rousing

When Democracy Suffers

"You Just Teach Silly Things"

A Good STEM Education is a Play-Based One

(Note: I hate that I need to write this chapter, just as I hated that I needed to write about how children learn to read in the next chapter. Play is a pure good and should not need to be defended, but I also know we live in a real world where policy-makers still consider play a mere relief from serious work rather than a core aspect of the real work of being human. I hope, at least, that those who do need to defend play will find this useful.)

My wife has been the CEO of a software company. Earlier in her career, she was an automotive executive and has held senior positions in several technology-based businesses. She is, as she realized to her delight not long ago, one of those much sought-for rarities: a woman with a successful STEM career. That said, she studied languages at university. That's right, languages, not science, technology, engineering, or math, yet here she is today running a technology company.

Science, technology, engineering, and math, or STEM as they are collectively called in the contemporary lexicon, has become an emphasis for our schools, both public and private. The idea is that those legendary "jobs of tomorrow" will require STEM skills, and so we are feverishly "educating" our children to be prepared for their future roles in the economy. Setting aside the hubris embodied in the assumption that anyone can predict what jobs our preschoolers will grow up to hold, science, technology, engineering, and math are important aspects of what it means to be human and fully worthy of exploration whether or not one is going to one day require specific employment skills.

Science, after all, is the grown-up word for play. As N.V.

Scarfe wrote while discussing Einstein, "The highest form of research is essentially play." I know a number of scientists, and whenever they are discussing their work, they describe it as play: "I was playing with the data, and guess what I discovered," or, "I played with the variables, and you won't believe what I found." Conversely, the highest form of play is essentially science, as children ask and answer their own questions with both rigor and joy without the soul-sucking artifice of rote.

Technology, which is the application of scientific knowledge for practical purposes, is how children typically extend their play, building upon their discoveries to further explore their world.

Engineering is the process by which children create their technologies, be they dams intended to hold back flowing water or springboards designed for jumping into it.

And math is something humans have to be taught to hate because, after all, it is the process of learning increasingly complex and wonderful ways to do things that give us great pleasure as human animals: patterning, classifying, and sorting. When we boil it down, that's the entirety of math, which is ultimately the foundation of analytical thinking.

The tragedy of STEM education in the early years, however, is that too many practitioners have concluded that we must engage in extraordinary measures to teach it, that without lectures, worksheets, and drill-and-kill testing, it simply won't happen, which is, in the lexicon of a generation long before mine, pure hogwash.

STEM education is not a complicated thing. Children are already doing it when we leave them alone to pursue their own interests in a lovely, varied, and stimulating environment. We can, however, destroy their love of science, technology, engineering, and math by turning it into the sort of rote learning that involves authoritarian adults dictating what, how, and by when particular knowledge is to be acquired or skills learned. A good STEM education, at least in the early years, is a play-based one; one that takes advantage of a child's natural curiosity; that gives free rein to their boundless capacity for inventiveness; and that understands that vocational training is but a small part of what an education should be about.

When we step back and really observe children in their "natural habitat," which is while playing, we can see the STEM learning, although it takes some practice because it's intertwined with the other important things they're working on like social-emotional skills, literacy, and the capacity for working with others, which is, at bottom, the most important "job" skill of all. Indeed, while we are only guessing at what STEM skills our preschoolers are going to need in the future, we do know that getting along with our fellow humans is the real secret to future employment, not to mention happiness.

When my wife was a preschooler, no one envisioned computers on every desktop, let alone on every laptop. The internet hadn't even made an appearance in science fiction novels. And we all carried dimes in our pockets just in case we needed to make a call on a public phone. Today, she is the CEO of a software company by way of the automotive industry by way of the jobs that her study of languages made available to her when she stepped into the workforce. The problem with predicting what specific "job" skills our children will need in the future is that we can only guess, because it's not us, but the children themselves who will invent those jobs, just as my wife has invented her own STEM career.

That said, when we allow children to explore their world through play, we see that they are already scientists, technologist, engineers, and mathematicians. We don't create them, but rather allow the time and space in which those natural drives can flourish, and that's how we ultimately insure that our children not only have the narrow skills that may or may not be necessary for those jobs of tomorrow, but also for the broader purpose of living a good life.

"But How Do They Learn to Read?"

"But how do they learn to read?"

It's the question most often asked by doubters when first learning about play-based education. Most people "get" that play is important for young children, at least to a certain degree—they're not ogres—but they just can't get their minds around the idea that most children, when left to their own devices, will actually learn to read without adult intervention.

First of all, from a purely developmental perspective, preschool-aged children should not be expected to be reading. This isn't to say that some preschoolers don't teach themselves to read. I've known readers as young as two. And at any given moment, there will be a handful of four- and five-year-olds at Woodland Park who are reading books on their own because that's how human development works: some children start speaking at three months, and some barely utter a word until after they've celebrated their fourth birthday; some are walking by six months, and some aren't up on their feet until they're closer to two. Parents might worry, but the truth is that it all falls well within the range of "normal." The research on reading indicates that the natural window for learning to read extends to as late as eleven years old!

Of course, in today's America, a child who is not reading by the time he is seven or eight is thought to have some sort of learning disability, when the fact is that he is likely perfectly normal. A couple years back, a University of Cambridge team reviewed all the available research on the topic and concluded that "formal" schooling should be delayed until children are at least seven, and that, indeed, pushing it earlier is damaging children's "academic" achievement, especially when it comes to reading.

> Studies have compared groups of children...who started formal literacy lessons at ages 5 and 7... (T)he early introduction of formal learning approaches to literacy does not improve children's reading development, and may be damaging. By the age of 11 there was no difference in reading ability level between the two groups, but the children who stared at 5 developed less positive attitudes to reading, and showed poorer text comprehension than those children who had started later.

Their recommendation is that the best "academic" education for children under seven is the sort of "informal, play-based" environment we offer at Woodland Park because that is how the human animal is designed to build the foundation for all future learning.

The sickening thing is that today's kindergartens and preschools are charging pell-mell in the wrong direction. A new University of Virginia study found that kindergarten changed in disturbing ways from 1999–2006. There was a marked decline in exposure to social studies, science, music, art, and physical education, and an increased emphasis on reading instruction. Teachers reported spending as much time on reading as all other subjects combined.

With the advent of the Common Core federal public school curriculum in the US (and it is a curriculum despite its advocates' insistence that they are merely "standards"), with its narrow focus on literacy, mathematics, and testing, it has gotten even worse since 2006. Indeed, according to the *New York Times*:

> Last year, average math scores…declined; reading scores were flat or decreased compared with a decade earlier.

We are proving the research: we are damaging our children. This is why I remain so consistently opposed to what is happening in our public schools. By law, I'm a mandatory reporter of child abuse in my state. This might not fit the legal definition, but it definitely fits the moral one.

That still begs the original question: how will they learn to read?

As I learned from Carol Black's brilliant essay entitled *A Thousand Rivers*, when Johannes Gutenberg invented the printing press in 1439, very few people could read. I must reiterate that, in fact, reading was primarily the domain of the clergy who needed the skill to read and create Bibles. But the printing press suddenly made printed matter widely available. With no notion of formal literacy education, Europeans were left to learn to read on their own, passing on the knowledge from one person to the next, from one generation to the next.

Literacy rates steadily climbed for the next couple hundred years, then surged around the time of the American Revolution when Thomas Payne's pamphlet *Common Sense* became a runaway hit, selling over a half million copies and going through twenty-five printings in its first year. It's estimated that 2.5 million colonists read it, an astronomical number for the time. And it's not easy reading. Nevertheless, historians credit this viral document with inspiring the thirteen American colonies to ultimately declare their independence from British rule.

People wanted to read, they *needed* to read, so they learned to read, which is why literacy rates in those original thirteen colonies were actually higher than those we see today in our fifty states. A similar thing has happened, albeit at a faster pace, with computer technology. I have a distinct memory of Dad buying an Apple II Plus, a machine that came with no software. Instead it came with thick instruction manuals that taught us how to write our own programs. You could take classes on "how to work your computer." Today, our two-year-olds are teaching themselves as these technology skills have gone viral. The idea of a computer class today is laughable, just as a reading class would have been laughable in 1776.

And just as "walking" or "talking" classes would be laughable to us today, so too should this whole nonsense of "reading" classes. Yet, shockingly, we continue to go backwards with literacy to the point that most of us seem to think that it's necessary that children spend days and years of their lives at earlier and earlier ages, being drilled in a utilitarian skill that past generations just learned, virally, over the natural course of living their lives. No wonder children hate school. No wonder they are bored and stressed out.

Certainly, there are children in our world who are "at risk" for not learning to read, including those with actual learning disabilities, as opposed to the manufactured ones we are currently slapping on normal children who are simply taking a little longer to getting around to reading. And for those children, as well as for those who are being raised in illiterate households, intervention may be necessary. But for the overwhelming majority of our children, the greatest literacy challenge they face is our obsessive rush for more and more earlier and earlier. We are, in our abject ignorance, our refusal to actually look at the evidence, teaching our children to hate reading, which is, in my view, a crime not only against children, but against all humanity.

Don't Buy the "Falling Behind" Snake Oil

What would you think if you saw a mother hovering over her two-month-old infant drilling her on vowel sounds? Or how about a father coaching his five-month-old on the finer points to walking? I expect you would think they were at best wasting their time. Two-month-olds can't talk, and five-month-olds can't walk, let alone be taught. Talking and walking are things children just learn. Now imagine that when these babies failed to acquire these capabilities that are clearly beyond their developmental grasp, these parents began to fret that their child was "falling behind." You would think they were crazy. If a doctor told these parents their child was "falling behind," we would think he was either incompetent or cruel.

Sadly, there are actually people out there doing things like this, hucksters who assert that babies can be taught to read, and there are devices on the market that purport to help babies learn to walk. The good news is that while there are some naive parents who fall for such gimmickry in the misguided attempt to somehow one-up nature's long, successful history of "teaching" talking and walking according to well-established developmental timelines, most of us know better than to worry about these things that virtually every child learns without any special interventions.

My own daughter spoke her first word at three months old, consistently saying "Papa" when I played and cared for her: she was putting together full sentences before six months. This same "advanced" child didn't crawl until her first birthday and wasn't walking until close to twenty months, a full lifetime "behind" some of her peers. Today, as you might expect, she talks and walks like the rest of the young adults: if she was ever behind, she caught up, and if she was ever ahead, the others caught up with her.

This unsavory practice of taking advantage of new-parent insecurities in the name of profit is one that deserves to be called out wherever it rears its nasty head, and it's borderline criminal when they play the "falling behind" card, which is why I'm writing today.

I've had the opportunity these past few years to travel around the world to talk to teachers and parents. Every place I go, I find myself discussing this bizarre notion of "school readiness." Often translated in the US as "kindergarten readiness," it is essentially code for reading. It seems that the powers that be in our respective nations have decided to sell parents on the snake oil that if your child isn't starting to read by five years old, she is "falling behind." They are doing this despite the fact that *every single legitimate study* ever done on the subject recommends that formal literacy education (if we *ever* even need it) not begin until a child is seven or eight years old. They are telling parents and teachers that children are "falling behind" despite the fact that *every single legitimate study* ever done finds that there are no long-term advantages to being an early reader, just as there are no long-term advantages to being early talkers or walkers. In fact, many studies have found that when formal literacy instruction begins too early, like at five, children grow up to be less motivated readers and less capable of comprehending what they've read. That's right, if anything, this "school readiness" fear-mongering may well turn out to be outright malpractice.

But the worst thing, the unforgivable thing, is the cruelty of the assertion that five-year-olds are "falling behind." It's one thing when commercial interests attempt to move their crappy merchandise by playing on fears, but when schools are doing it, when teachers are doing it, that's unconscionable. I'm a staunch supporter of my fellow teachers, but I am calling my colleagues out on this one. Teachers should know better than to help these guys sell this stuff: it's bad for kids, it's bad for families, and it's bad for society. We are the professionals. Teachers need to put our collective foot down, point to the research, rely on our own experiences, and if we can't refuse to subject young children to developmentally inappropriate, potentially harmful "readiness" garbage for fear of losing our jobs, the least we can do is refuse to take part in the crass abusiveness of "falling behind." If we can't do that, maybe we don't deserve to call ourselves professionals.

The Evidence Tells Us We Should Set Kids Free

Few things have put more wear and tear on my teeth than the entire concept of "teaching" character traits like "grit," "resilience," "optimism," "conscientiousness," and "self-control." It's not that those things aren't important. Indeed, they are vital, not just for academic achievement, but for any kind of real, lasting success, be it in school, work, or just being a member of a family or community. No, what sets my teeth grinding is the self-satisfied way in which so-called education reformers, the ones with a product or agenda to sell, insist that they have figured out how to "teach" these things, even going so far as to produce pre-packaged curricula they claim will do this.

It's classic snake oil, based upon the faith-based notion that all these kids need are more lectures, more tests (yes, there are actually standardized tests now that purport to measure these noncognitive traits), and a vigorous system of rewards and punishments. It has been these Skinnerian notions that have led to such things as zero-tolerance policies, No Child Left Behind, Race to the Top, and other anti-child measures, none of which have worked in any way to move the needle on the holy grail of "academic achievement." It hasn't worked because what they are doing is not based upon science, but rather an ideology that comes right out of neoliberal economic theory—the kind business executives, the very folks who are leading the charge to turn our schools into test-score coal mines, tend to favor.

To underline this point, Roland G. Fryer, Jr., an economics professor at Harvard, distributed nearly $10 million in cash incentives (e.g., rewards) to students in several US cities over the course of several years, with the idea of improving reading scores. These came in the form of cash, cell phones, and other inducements just to read books and spend more time on math homework. The results: "Students performed the tasks necessary to get paid, but their average math scores at the end of eight months hadn't changed at all…their reading scores…actually went *down*."

This quote is from an article by education author Paul Tough, who appeared in *The Atlantic* entitled "How Kids Really Succeed," in which he contrasts actual brain research with current educational practices. It's a worthwhile read, especially the first half where he discusses the impact of early childhood "toxic stress" on the ability to learn. What researchers are concluding is that the behaviorists are wrong, at least with regard to children:

> (W)e are mostly motivated not by the material consequences of our actions but by the inherent enjoyment and meaning that those actions bring us, a phenomenon called intrinsic motivation.

This brings a resounding, "Well, of course," from those of us who work with young children.

> (Researchers) identified three key human needs—our need for *competence*, our need for *autonomy*, and our need for relatedness, meaning *personal connection*—and they posited that intrinsic motivation can be sustained only when we feel that those needs are being satisfied. (Emphasis added by me.)

Competence, autonomy, and personal connection: these are the building blocks of a play-based education, where children are allowed to become competent by having the time and space to autonomously ask and answer their own questions within the context of a loving community. This is where those bedrock character traits come from. And it is why they will never emerge from the reward-and-punishment model of the neoliberal Skinnerians.

Sadly, when Tough asks the question, "So what do these academic environments look like?" (e.g., those that emphasize competence, autonomy, and personal connection) he answers it by going into normal schools where teachers are using this research to manipulate kids into "learning" what adults have pre-determined is good for the kids, rather than what the kids themselves are driven to pursue, which means they might produce statistically significant improvements, but ones that are still marginal compared to the sort that would come from the kind of systemic change that brain (and psychological and anthropological and pedagogical) research tells us would transform the lives of not just young children, but all of us.

The evidence tells us that we should set kids free to lead their own learning, but the policy-makers (and in that I include most of us as well) are still fixated on getting those damned orcas to jump just a little higher so that we adults can applaud ourselves for knowing what's best for them.

"Teach by Doing Whenever You Can"

I reckon it would be best if we didn't put so much energy into worrying about our children's futures. It would be best for both us and our kids if we could more often just be here in the present with them, wondering who they are right now, appreciating the unique human they already are, helping and loving them right now. That would be best, but human parents have never been very good at it. Sometimes we dream big dreams for them, imagining our children, their best qualities flourishing, as masterful something or others, admired, inspired, passionate, and supremely comfortable in their own skins. But there are times when we fear their worst qualities and fret that they will grow to be spoiled, disrespectful, and lazy, prone to messy bedrooms, selfishness, depression or worse.

Example is the school of mankind, and they will learn by no other. ~Edmund Burke

These thoughts enter our heads because we are the adults, cursed with the disease of thinking we have any control over the future. Maybe, we think, if we just lecture our children enough, take them to church often enough, give them enough chores to do, and reward and punish them appropriately, we can somehow stave off the bad future and encourage the good. But that isn't the way it works.

Most of what children learn about being a human being in this world, they learn from the people they most love, but not because they have been drilled, scolded, or otherwise indoctrinated, but rather because they follow their examples.

If we want children to be kind, we must be kind. If we want them to be tidy, we must be tidy. If we want them to be respectful, then we must be respectful, especially toward them. Indeed, the more we focus on ourselves, on being the people we want ourselves to be, the better we "teach" the most important life lessons. Our children will not learn to pursue their passions unless the loving adults in their lives set that example for them. They will not learn to be unselfish if we live with tight fists. They will not learn to manage their emotions if their role models haven't figured it out for themselves.

Teach by doing whenever you can, and only fall back upon words when doing it is out of the question.
~Jean-Jacques Rousseau

That's asking a lot of adults, I know, but if we are going to ask it of our children, we must also ask it of ourselves. And we must also know that we will fail in our role modeling and fail often, but in that, too, we are role models. Children do not expect their parents to be perfect, but they are always making a careful study of what we do when we make mistakes. Do we give up? Do we blame others? Do we rant and rave? Do we cry and mope? Or are we able to apologize, forgive ourselves, and get back up to try again? The approach we take is very likely the approach our children will, in turn, grow to embrace as their own.

Teaching is painful, continual, and difficult work to be done by kindness, by watching, and by praise, but above all by example.
~John Ruskin

Of course, we all know examples of children, perhaps even ourselves, who have overcome poor role modeling. Perhaps we eat healthier than our own parents, or make more time for our own kids, or avoid committing felonies. But even then, it is the example they set more than the lesson they "taught" that informed our future.

No one can predict the future, and only fools take their attempts to do so seriously. When we are hopeful about the future, we are, as my wife and I like to say, just "spending Yugoslavian dollars." When we worry, we are, at best, wasting valuable emotional bandwidth that would be better applied to right now. The only future we can predict with any certainty is the next ten minutes, and I've found it's generally not too hard to be the best me, the person I most want to be, for the next ten minutes. When we can do that, ten minutes at a time, we are being the teacher—the parent—our child most needs. And it is from those ten-minute building blocks that the future emerges.

A master can tell you what he expects of you. A teacher, though, awakens your own expectations. ~Patricia Neal

It's not our job to "teach" our children anything, but rather to love them and to strive to live according to our own expectations, not in the past or future, but right now. The future, as it always does, will take care of itself.

Too Many "Tripping Hazards"

A while back, a concerned person took a look at our junk-yard playground, tsk-tsk-ed, and handed me a brochure on playground safety. Her leading objection was that our space presented too many "tripping hazards," as if the world is not one giant tripping hazard. I did take the brochure seriously enough to track down the citations, which ultimately led me to a concerned parents group from back in the 1980s that, without concerning itself with any studies, data, or research, had come up with a set of playground safety standards that had grown from their ability to imagine the worst-case scenario. What I normally refer to as catastrophic thinking.

I ultimately accommodated this person by agreeing to ask a parent to kick loose things off the walkways at the end of the day.

We've been playing on our school's junkyard playground for a long time now. I don't know if it qualifies as a proper "adventure playground" or not, but I tend think of it as a preschool version of one. We've had some bumped heads and skinned knees, of course, but we've only once sent a kid to the doctor's office. Indeed, the boy had tripped, but it was over his own feet, and one of his teeth pierced his upper lip, requiring stitches. According to the child's mother, the doctor who attended him called it "one of the most common childhood injuries."

Not long ago, I came across a fascinating study (an actual study, not just catastrophic thinking) in which a private school in Texas decided to compare the injury rates between its conventional playground with its out-of-the-box, up-to-standards play structures, and its adventure playground, the one with "timber structures, tools, junk materials, and skilled workers." They found what those of us who have watched children play in both kinds of places have always observed: despite the apparent "tripping hazards," there were fewer injuries on the adventure playground.

Now, in fairness, neither playground was particularly dangerous. The injury rate on the standard-issue playground was about the same as a child playing at home, while the rate of injury on the adventure playground was similar to playing ping pong. Still, it's nice to have some actual data to support what those of us in the business already suspect, which is always better than relying upon someone else's catastrophic thinking.

As If Mathematics Was Coded into Our Genes

The young two-year-old had carried the plastic bears halfway across the room to show me. "Blue bears," he said, holding them in front of his own eyes.

I said, "Two blue bears." He looked from one to the other, then pushed them a bit closer to me, as if to say, *Look at them.* I said again, "Two blue bears."

He looked from one to the other again, then held them closer together, right in front of his eyes. There was something else he wanted to say about those bears, but he was struggling to find the words.

"You are really looking at those bears."

He said, "Blue bears," and pushed them toward my eyes, as if asking me to really look as well.

I really looked. I said, "You are showing me two blue bears. One of them is darker blue, and one of them is lighter blue." He looked at them, examining them, then shoved them toward me again. I said, "You are showing me two blue bears that are different shades of blue." That's when he smiled.

"Different," he said. "Blue bears different." He then took them back with him halfway across the room.

I followed him to where the kids were playing with the little plastic bears, plastic baskets, and water. One boy held an empty basket. He picked up a bear as it floated past, putting it in his basket.

He beamed at me as I knelt beside him, so I replied, "You put a bear in your basket."

He put another bear in his basket, then another, each time, smiling at me. When he put the fourth bear in the basket, he told me, "More."

I answered, "You have more bears in your basket."

He then added another and another, each time telling me, "More," "More," "More."

Later, I was leaning over the top of some cabinets, watching the two-year-olds playing with our wooden trains. Children were queuing their train cars up, the way one does, one after another.

A girl shouted, "Teacher Tom, look at my long train!" I looked at it. She connected another car and shouted, "Teacher Tom, my train is longer!" I nodded. She added another and another, each time proclaiming it longer until there were no more train cars in her immediate vicinity. She then announced, "It's the longest!"

I was still leaning across the shelves when another girl brought me a wooden tree that came with one of the intermixed train sets we own. She set it in front of me.

I said, "You brought me a tree." She picked up another tree. I said, "Now I have two trees." Then another. "Now I have three threes." And another. "Now I have four trees." The trees were of different colors, shapes, and manufactures, but they were all trees. Then she added a small traffic sign. I looked at her in mock confusion, and she laughed and laughed at the math prank she'd just pulled on me.

This is what preschool mathematics looks like in a play-based environment. It is not an academic pursuit, but rather a truly intellectual one, even a joyful one, something every child pursues as if it was coded into her genes. And indeed it is.

How a Junkyard Playground Works

She hadn't come looking for me, but when I passed where she played with a friend, she said, "Teacher Tom, look at our play area." They then gave me a tour of junk they had purposefully arranged, explaining to me how everything worked. There was a slide and a merry-go-round and several other things that adult play-area designers haven't yet, and probably never will, invent.

After admiring their project for a bit, a project that was still in process, I made my way up the hill to where the "bad guy" trap had taken up residence. This was a well-established project, undertaken mostly by a partnership of two boys, that had literally been months in the making.

I kept expecting them to lose interest, but they persisted in their project week after week. It had been disassembled, partially and totally, by other children several times, but they rebuilt it again and again, each time bigger and better than before. Every single piece of junk in their construction had a purpose, and they happily explained those purposes to anyone who showed an interest.

Not far from the "bad buy" trap, some girls were playing "birds." It was a game that one of them had been playing at least since the previous year, but lately her passion for the game had inspired her playmates. Normally, their game involved chirping, flapping, and jumping off of things to simulate flying, but on this day, they had built something from the junk at hand.

They had arranged orange traffic cones atop a small hill, surrounding what was left of an old shipping crate. "It's our nest, Teacher Tom."

There was a kind of gangway, so I asked, "Is this how you get in?"

"No, this is the kids' nest. The trampoline is where the adults sleep. The wood is how we get to each other's rooms. *Tweet, tweet, tweet, tweet.*" They then went on to explain the purpose of everything in their nest built with junk.

Then, down at the workbench, I found a pair of brothers using PVC pipe to build a "machine" that performed such miraculous feats that they couldn't even explain it.

Our junkyard playground was in full swing, with every corner being used for purposeful collaboration and deep, meaningful play, to a level that no adult could have imagined, although some might find echoes in their childhood memories.

"Play with a Purpose"

A few years back, I was watching a boy named Henry carry a yellow traffic pylon across the playground. He carefully placed it on the ground, not on its base, but on its side, taking care to get it "just so" before climbing atop an old packing crate. He stood poised atop the crate for a moment, then launched himself, coming down on the pylon. *Crack!* I heard the sound of the pylon breaking from across the yard.

Stupidly, I asked him, "Henry, why did you do that?"

Without missing a beat, he replied, "I wanted to see if I could break it." Duh.

We had a brief conversation about property after that, although in hindsight, I think that "property" has a somewhat different meaning when we spend our time on a junkyard playground like ours, but I keep this episode in mind whenever people begin to talk about "play with a purpose," a mantra for those who have accepted the importance of play while clinging to the hubristic notion that children need adults to "make" it educational. Here was a boy with a question, one of his own devising, and therefore one in which he had a genuine interest. He was motivated by his curiosity. *Can I break this?* So he set up an experiment in which he discovered his answer.

The standard definitions of play frame it as "for enjoyment" or "recreation," which can clearly both be aspects of play, but those of us who spend our lives observing children going about the business of actually playing, know that there is always a question behind what they do, even if it's not one that can be stated as clearly as Henry's. The purpose of the player isn't always evident to the observer, but there is always, beneath the enjoyment or recreation, an inquiry of some sort at work, one that might not always lead to a definitive answer, as Henry's experiment did, but is an exploration of oneself, the other people, and both the physical and psychological environment in which the child finds herself. Play is how our instinct to educate ourselves manifests.

When it comes to education, play is enough: it contains within it all the important questions and answers. We don't need adults commanding, coaxing, coaching, or cajoling the children in order for it to be purposeful. When I hear people use the phrase "play with a purpose" (or something similar), I cringe because no matter how well intended, I know that these are people who don't trust the children's natural instincts and so feel compelled, however gently, to turn their self-directed learning into yet another adult-directed activity that may or may not lead children to answers that are important to them.

Not long ago, I watched a teacher attempt to compel a group of five-year-olds through a type of relay race she had designed to help the children "deepen" their understanding of the autumn leaves they had collected, matching like-with-like and so on. The teacher's enthusiasm and the children's curiosity about this "game" she was describing was enough to keep them interested for a few minutes as they waited in queues for their turn to race from one end of the room to the other, but it wasn't long before there were children exploring under tables, chatting with friends, and, in the case of one boy, simply moping against the wall. The teacher started by trying to cheerfully coax them all back into the game, but it didn't take. She tried to ignore the rebellions to focus on the children who were still engaged in her play-with-a-purpose game, although it seemed to me that most of them were doing it by way of pleasing their teacher more than because the game held their interest. I sympathized with the teacher as I watched her jaw twitch, because I have experienced similar episodes in my own teaching past, but the bottom line is that she had managed to turn their natural interest in things like collecting fall leaves and running into a chore from which none of them were learning much other than perhaps a lesson in obedience and disobedience.

Children's play is always purposeful, even if we can't tell what that purpose is, and it's always educational, even if we don't know what they are learning. The moment the adult imposes her own agenda, play comes to an end, no matter how playful their top-down agenda tries to be. Children will always lose interest because the questions are not their own, and without interest, "learning" becomes a chore for everyone.

Play is a pure good, like love or happiness, and, like love or happiness, it tends to disappear when we overthink it.

My Adult Sense of Justice

When I was a new parent, my mother told me, "All young children want from adults is attention. They don't care if it's positive or negative, so you might as well give them the attention you want to give them, because otherwise they'll take it from you, and you're not going to like how they do that."

A few years ago, a boy named River was just milling around while most of his classmates were busy putting Duplos into their plastic tubs. On any given day, there are always one or two kids who opt out of the project of tidying up the classroom. With my mom's advice in mind, I tried to ignore him, focusing my attention instead on the children who were engaged. There was a time when I might have made the effort to try to coax or cajole him into participating, but I'd learned through experience that if that's where I put my attention, that's where the rest of the kids would want to be, so instead I tried to ignore him, even as his non-involvement offended my adult sense of justice.

Whenever I talk or write about how we handle clean-up time at Woodland Park, people ask what we do about those who decline to participate. The short answer is nothing. I tend to let them go about their business as long as they aren't impeding those of us who are taking care of the classroom. That's what I did in River's case, asking him to move when he got in someone's way, but otherwise staying relentlessly focused on the children putting those Duplos into the boxes.

"Robert is putting away the Duplos super fast."

"Missy is looking under the cabinets for Duplos."

"Pat and Owen are working together."

"This is our school, and we're taking care of it."

Before long, the first of the plastic tubs was filled. That's when River sprang into action, leaping in from the sidelines to assertively snap a lid on the box, then snatching it away from the others to carrying it to its shelf. Again, my adult sense of justice was roused. *That's not fair*, I thought. *The other kids did all the work and he stole their glory.* None of the kids complained, but it irked me. Then, the following day, he did the same thing, so in the interest of "protecting" the rights of the other kids, the ones who had done all the work, I decided I was going to try to prevent another repeat. On the following day, when I saw him once more avoiding the "hard work," I engaged him quietly off to the side, hoping to give the other kids the opportunity to experience the satisfaction of snapping the lids onto the boxes they had diligently filled.

As I whispered to him, we were interrupted by one of the other kids who insisted upon handing River the lid to the tub. I looked up to see the rest of the kids standing around it, waiting for him to do the honors.

You see, instead of being resentful of River, they had come to accept that it was his clear and proper job to snap the lids onto the full boxes. It was my adult sense of justice that caused me to think something was wrong, whereas the kids harbored no ill-feelings. Indeed, they saw him as essential.

So yes, on any given day, there are two or three kids who don't pull their own weight, but it's not been a problem since I've learned to set aside my adult sense of justice and simply ignore them, while focusing my attention on those who do. Perhaps the kids will one day develop this adult idea of justice, but I sort of hope not. In many ways, their concept of fairness is much more evolved than ours.

"It's Not a Drum"

As clean-up time approached, I began to survey the two-year-olds. "Is it clean-up time?" Some said, "Yes," while others informed me that they wanted to wait "Three minutes" or "Five minutes." They all knew by now that after we tidied up, we went outside. I had never instructed the children to participate in cleaning up, but I had instructed the parent-teachers in this cooperative class to practice stepping back, to leave space for the children who choose to participate to do so in a meaningful way.

After three or five minutes, I retrieved the hand drum we use as a transition signal. Children were engaged in their play all around the room, although a couple of them stopped what they were doing to notice me.

I said, "I'm getting the clean-up-time banjo," and proceeded to "play" it like a banjo. A few more kids noticed me. "It's not a banjo," I said. "It's a flute," and I played the drumstick like a flute. "It's not a flute. It's a trumpet." I played the stick like a trumpet. Now, several more children were watching me.

One of them laughed, saying, "It's a drum!"

"It's not a trumpet." I continued, "It's a trombone," and I pantomimed playing the stick as a trombone.

"It's not a trombone, Teacher Tom! It's a drum!" By now, about half the kids had dropped what they were doing to watch me.

"It's not a trombone, it's a tuba." I used the drumstick for the mouthpiece and held the drum over my head to represent the large, flared tuba bell.

By now, most of the kids were paying attention, and most

of them had come over to where I stood on our checker-board rug amidst the blocks that were scattered there. Several of them shouted at me, "It's a drum!" and, "It's not a tuba!"

I said, "It's not a tuba, it's a harp."

"It's not a harp!" they shouted. "It's a drum!" Some were so full of anticipation that they demanded, "Bang it!"

"It's not a harp, it's a piano."

"*It's a drum!*"

"*Bang it!*"

"It's not a piano, it's a drum, and I'm going to bang it so loud that your brains are going to shoot out of your ears and splat on the wall."

By now, everyone was focused on my silly little show, and they were demanding that I bang the drum. They were demanding the transition. It was not the first time I had done this; indeed, it's a regular part of my teaching repertoire. After a couple of goofs where I pretended to miss the drum, I finally made contact, playing it gently with three soft beats because they were all so focused with anticipation that that was all I needed.

As I said, I had never suggested that these two-year-olds participate in clean-up, although many of them had been pitching in of their own accord. On this day, however, the sound of blocks being dropped into boxes was almost deafening, as they all, as one, leapt to the task. There were a couple visitors in the room at the time, mothers touring the school with an eye toward enrolling for next year. The response was so dramatic, so instantaneous, so opposite of the stereotype we have of young children, that I couldn't help making eye-contact with one of the prospective parents boastfully, as if to non-verbally say, *Surely, you want your kid to be a part of this!*

I then continued to make informational statements like, "That box needs to go over here," and "Phillip is putting away lots of blocks," and "We need help at the red table," until everything was packed away. None of them complained. None of them hid. None of them sought to avoid the "work." They simply did what we were doing until it was done, then we put on our coats and went outside.

How I Would Start to Transform Public Education

I often write as a critic of normal schools, with their compulsory top-down, standardized curricula that devalue the interests of our youngest citizens in favor of adults deciding what, when, and how children are to learn. It's a system that flies in the face of what we know about how human beings are designed to learn, a product of the Industrial Revolution that has continued more or less unchanged to this day, perpetuated by habit rather than an ongoing, rigorous application of the science. The evidence is clear that if we truly want well-educated citizens, ones capable of thinking for themselves, of questioning authority, of standing up for their beliefs and values, people who are sociable, motivated, and able to work well with others, then we would have long ago transformed our schools into places where children direct their own learning.

Sometimes I like to imagine what that would mean. More and more Americans are opting out altogether, choosing a version of homeschooling or un-schooling that works for their families. Others have sought out alternative private schools that employ, say, the Waldorf method or Reggio Emilia or perhaps even the democratic free-school model of places like the Sudbury Valley School. These are all fine ways for individuals to opt out of normal public education, but there is a limit to how many of us can afford the price, either in terms of time or money. No, it seems to me that a real transformation of education in America, one that includes *all* children, must be a public one: well-educated citizens are a public good, one that is vital to every citizen in that it is the only guarantee of our grand experiment in self-governance. So, what I'm thinking about here is a true trans-formation of *public* education, which, I believe, is necessary if our democracy is to continue to thrive.

If we get rid of schools as we know them, it seems to me that we will still need something "like" schools, safe places for our children to spend their days. Unless this transformation in education comes as a part of a wider transformation in our society, one that does not require so many two-income families, "schools" will need to continue to serve this function. Indeed, I reckon that the school facilities that we've already built will work just fine as a starting point: large buildings with lots of room and, typically, with a fairly substantial amount of land surrounding them.

Neighborhood children of all ages would arrive at these "schools" in the mornings just as they do today and, as in the democratic free-school model, they would be free to pursue their own interests throughout the day with the support of "teachers," whose jobs would be re-defined to more closely resemble that of professional play-workers, adults who spend their days loitering with intent, not intervening or directing, but available to step in, minimally, when needed.

There would, of course, continue to be the cafeteria, a place where professional cooks prepare and serve meals, the difference being that these kitchens would be open to the children to participate as their age and interests (e.g., chopping, stirring, measuring, serving) develop under the guidance of the kitchen staff. Likewise, there would be a garden and greenhouse tended by professional gardeners charged with supplying the kitchen, and who would also likewise make room for children interested in any or all aspects of that process. There would be a functioning workshop where professional carpenters would build the furniture and other items needed by the school, another place where children of all ages are welcome. These transformed schools would be home to musicians and other artists, mechanics, engineers, computer scientists, psychologists, athletes, handy(wo)men, nurses, custodians, accountants, yoga masters, and other specialists, each going about their real work while also always making space for young apprentices of all ages, role-modeling, supporting, and teaching, allowing the children to explore as their ages and interests dictate.

But, of course, the children would not be limited. If a group of kids take an interest in, for instance, building a rocket, the more experienced children (which would likely most often be the oldest, but not always) would lead, while the adults would be there to help with locating information or securing materials.

These "schools" would not just be for children. Neighborhood seniors, for instance, would also be invited on campus to spend all or part of their days, sharing their skills and wisdom, while also participating in meals and serving as audiences for dramatic and musical performances. In the evenings, parents would be encouraged to not just fetch their kids and rush off, but to rather spend their evenings there, together with other families, dining, dancing, reading in the library, or puttering around the workshop or garden, and otherwise hanging out with their neighbors, creating community.

Each neighborhood school would be "owned" by the neighborhood, in the way that our cooperative school is owned by the parents who enroll their children. Each household would have an equal voice in how their school operates, managing the funds to best serve their community, democratically creating a school that most perfectly reflects the aspirations and dreams of the people who live there.

These transformed schools would be, like our democracy itself, grand experiments, each one continually evolving to serve the needs and interests of the neighborhood, and especially the children. I envision them as standing at the hearts of their neighborhoods, around-the-clock gathering places, based not on commerce, but upon the shared interests of the people who live in the community: places that serve as models of real self-governance in action. I imagine that children who are raised in this type of environment will grow into the sorts of citizens we most need.

This is just a thumbnail of how I see transformed public education in America. There is so much more to talk about.

Meetings

It would be an exaggeration to say that I could count all the meetings I'd attended by the time I was nineteen years old on one hand, but not by a lot. I mean, there were those Cub Scout pack meetings where we sat in the church pews, and our baseball coaches often called it a "team meeting" when they sat us down in centerfield to lecture us, but those weren't meetings as I came to know them as an adult. We might have called them "meetings," but they were generally just one-way streets with adults standing in front of us lecturing.

In other words, these "meetings" were more or less like school, where we had all been taught to sit in our assigned seats, to only speak when questioned, and only then if our raised hands were selected. We were chastised for whispering, passing notes, cracking jokes, or getting up from our seats out of turn. We were even expected to ask permission to go to the toilet. Things loosened up a little in high school—as I recall, there were no assigned seats, for instance—but generally speaking, this was the nature of "meetings" up until, suddenly, we were out in the world where the "skills" we had worked so hard on developing over the course of the better part of two decades were made moot by reality.

In adult meetings, there are no assigned seats, and people whisper, pass notes, and crack jokes all the time. We leave our seats to go to the toilet, to get a coffee refill, or to run any number of other small "errands," including just pacing around in the back of the room when our legs start to cramp up. Heck, some people don't sit at all, instead choosing to lean against a wall, while others might, in more informal settings, opt to sit on the floor. Most of the time, we forgo hand raising altogether with folks chiming in as necessary, like in a conversation, but even when the group is large enough that we need to raise our hands, it's simply as a tool for making sure everyone gets to speak and be heard rather than as crowd control.

We too often expect more out of children than we expect from ourselves, and this is a good example. The only time during our Woodland Park school day that we expect all the children to convene is at circle time, our daily classroom meeting, which is fifteen to thirty minutes, typically during which we come together and practice being in a group, raising our voices together, engaging in discussion, making decisions, and telling stories. I know there are some play-based educators who treat these meetings as optional, but for us they form the backbone of our small democratic society. We do tend to raise hands, but not always, only when there are so many voices trying to be heard that we need a way to take turns. There are no assigned seats. Children can sit, kneel, or lie down. If they want to stand, we have designated the back of the room so as to avoid blocking the views of others. We practice whispering, should we have something to say to a friend. No one has to ask permission to use the toilet. In other words, we run our circle time like the meetings I attend as an adult, including setting the agenda.

I know that most of the children I teach will move on to more traditional schools, places where they will be expected to behave in ways that are rarely found outside of schools, and it's possible that their teachers will struggle with these kids who have grown accustomed to democracy, but I have no interest in preparing them for that. My job isn't to prepare children for school, but rather for life, and I will not hold children to standards that I don't live up to myself.

Transitions

Most kids I've known, most days, are eager to come to school, but some kids drag their feet every day, and all of them have mornings when they would rather not. I get it, and I don't take it personally. After all, I love my job, but I'm not always a happy camper about getting dressed and getting out the door either.

It's typically not about school, but rather about the transition. We've all known kids who struggle with transitions, and it isn't really something we necessarily outgrow. I mean, that's what Monday mornings are all about, right? Or returning from vacations. On the final night of the most recent winter holiday break, I found myself wishing for just one more day, and I have the best job in the world.

Children have their adults to push back against, and they do. They don't want to transition from the playground to go back home, they don't want to leave home to go to school, and nearly every day I hear kids whining at their parents that they don't want to leave school, even as their mothers are telling them that their next stop is the playground. As adults, there is typically no one but us to push back against, so we play games like hitting the snooze alarm, but ultimately it's our sense of responsibility rather than another person's scolding that gets us out of bed.

We all want our kids to be the sort who jump out of bed, dress themselves, make short work of breakfast, and are waiting at the door in plenty of time, but it's not in human nature to be eager to stop having fun in order to have fun. Indeed, one could argue that a strong resistance to transitions is part and parcel with feeling contented with how things are *right now*, which is a state of enlightenment. For instance, I love when I tell the kids that I'm thinking of banging the drum (our signal for clean-up time) and they call out for "five more minutes!" It means they are fully engaged. By the same token, I often feel like a bit of a failure when a kid prompts me, "Can you bang the drum now?"

Life is a series of transitions. Rarely are we in a position to let it just flow from one thing to the next, so all of us, whatever our natural temperament regarding transitions, learn our own ways to handle them. And young children, more often than not, start by targeting the obvious "villain," which is the adult who is telling her she must move on, which then turns into a power struggle that leaves no one feeling happy. If our goal is to give our kids the opportunity to develop their own sense of responsibility about life's necessary transitions, then it's important that we work to take the focus away from "mean Mommy" and onto the schedule itself.

Many parents find it useful to, in non-transitional moments, talk to their children in advance about the transitions they can expect in the coming hours, days, or even weeks, depending on their age, and then regularly remind them of the full schedule, including the unscheduled parts, throughout the day. All of us tend to do better when we know what to expect because it gives us the opportunity to prepare ourselves and develop our own philosophical approach to moving on from one thing to the next. Perhaps, most importantly, it allows children to begin to see that it's not Mommy or Daddy, but rather the schedule that makes the transition necessary.

And until we have the revolution, that's the way it's going to be. In the meantime, we learn our schedules, acknowledge our emotions, and hit the snooze alarm until our sense of responsibility gets us out of bed.

What It Means to Be Equal and Free

Very often, when those who live outside our progressive education bubble hear about our practices, their response is to envision a sort of chaotic mob rule, in which children are allowed to run wild. They warn of devastating consequences, of children who will grow into criminals or sociopaths, and that what we are doing will lead to a sort of tyranny of the children in which Hobbesian brutishness rules the day.

These are, of course, very similar to the arguments that have always been made against democracy, and by some accounts (but by no means all), these fears did come to pass to some extent when the ancient Athenians attempted to govern themselves through direct democracy, a form in which there is a danger that the will of the majority will trample the rights of a minority. Our founders were, of course, aware of this potential for "tyranny of the majority," and so when choosing what form of government to embody in our constitution, they went with a republic in which representatives are elected democratically. In other words, instead of a government directly controlled by the people, it is indirectly controlled: what dictionaries at the time defined as a "representative democracy." Encyclopedias have been written, and will continue to be written, discussing the nuances of the republic vs. democracy debate, one that I'd rather not engage in here, except to say that however you define our form of government, we are, together, attempting to self-govern with democracy as the centerpiece, and that, as it has been from the onset, is a grand experiment.

Similarly, our little cooperative preschool democracy is an experiment, one not bound by a constitution, but rather by the presence of loving adults. This is not, as some fear, an exercise in *laissez fair* parenting/teaching, but rather a laboratory in which we provide the space, tools, and autonomy in which children experiment with what it means to live among one another as equal and free citizens.

It is my view, one shared with our nation's founders, that a well-educated citizenry is the foundation of a democracy. The longer I've been a teacher, however, the more aware I become that our standard educational model, the one that emerged largely from the factory model of the Industrial Revolution, a model that supposes we need only fill those empty vessels with letters and numbers and dates, moving them along from grade to grade, is not up to the standards required for self-governance.

I believe we've lost sight of the promise of our nation. I cannot recall ever hearing an elected official speak of education in anything other than economic terms, and I have *never* heard one connect it to "life, liberty, and the pursuit of happiness." I rarely hear of our presidents or legislators spoken of as "representatives," but rather as "leaders." Voters stay away from polling places in droves, apathetic, let alone engaging in the day-to-day processes of democracy, not caring or perhaps not knowing how. Or worse, not feeling that they can or should have any impact on the civic life of our nation. We distrust and vilify government, painting it as a "them vs. us" conflict, and when I dare to point out that "them *is* us," I'm scornfully asked, "Where have you been hiding?"

The average citizen has withdrawn from the process of self-governance, leaving behind a vacuum that has been filled by political parties, corporate lobbyists, and radical partisans, who have taken us so far away from the promise of self-governance, that many of us, if not most, feel helpless in the face of it, withdrawing and wishing pox on the whole lot of them, castigating political discourse as base and impolite.

I teach the way I do because, I suppose, I'm an idealist. I do believe in the promise of day-to-day, retail self-government: the kind of government that is made up of friends and neighbors capable and willing to discuss the issues of the day over their back fences, in their churches, and while waiting in line at the supermarket. The kind of government in which we the people are capable and willing to listen, to debate, and to think for ourselves. I'm the kind of idealist who believes that schools should be preparing children to engage with one another as equal and free humans who are fully enfranchised.

I teach the way I do because I want the children who pass my way to have the opportunity, at least during their time with me, to practice what it means to be equal and free. In part, I write about it because I hope that others will be inspired to do the same. We are a young nation, and our experiment in democracy is only just getting under way. If we are to succeed, it won't be because some hero swoops in to save us, but rather because we decide we must do it together, day-to-day, thinking critically, speaking honestly, listening passionately, and acting as if we are, indeed, equal and free.

Rabble Rousing

We live in a time when there exists committees of men and women who come together to decide what our children should learn: what they should understand from the literature they read, what kinds of equations they should be able to solve, what scientific processes they'll need to know, which dates and important battles they must recite. These men and women in their collective wisdom pick and choose from the infinite universe those bits and pieces that will define what it is to be educated in this school or that school, in this district or that district, in this state or that state, and (I'm quite confident the effort is underway in this era of internationalization) in this nation or that nation. These committees determine not only *what* children are to learn, but *by when* they are to learn these things.

This committee-created standardization is then enforced through a system of "benchmarks," measured through high-stakes standardized tests that, bizarrely, focus almost exclusively on the even narrower areas of literacy and math. It's a system of dog-eat-dog competition, pitting teacher against teacher, school against school, district against district, and state against state in a winner-take-all cage match for funding and jobs.

It's happening, of course, with a propagandistic veneer of benevolence, even philanthropy, promoted by the promise of "serving students," a faux outrage about old methods that are failing us, the soaring rhetoric of egalitarianism, and with the strangest sight of all in our times, apparent political bipartisanship, bought and paid for by for-profit education corporations that have only just begun to raid the money that we the people have quite rightly set aside for the purpose of educating our children.

Needless to say, I do not believe that this situation "serves children," let alone democracy, which, as I complained of before, is *never* mentioned in any of our public discussions. These efforts to impose an anti-democratic, top-down, corporate-style super-hierarchy on our schools is quite explicitly an attempt to turn public education into a lucrative system of vocational training.

One of the main reasons I teach the way I do, and write about it, is that I want parents to be dissatisfied and suspicious of what is being planned for their children who are so much more than the rhetorical "workforce of tomorrow." I want teachers to feel frustrated and even outraged that if they are to truly serve the student in their classroom instead of the theoretical student proposed by these committees, they must do so subversively, and at the real risk of finding themselves on the street. I don't know what form it will take, but it increasingly looks to me like the push back will ultimately need to take the form of civil disobedience: a students' rights movement led by parents, teachers, and the students themselves.

That's right, one of the reasons I teach the way I do is because I'm a rabble rouser.

The history of progress in our nation is one of rabble rousing, of civil (and sometimes not-so-civil) disobedience. Thomas Jefferson correctly predicted that whenever things get so far wrong as to attract our notice, we could be relied upon to set them right, from the American Revolution right through our various civil and labor rights movements.

And I try very hard to not be a hypocrite about this. It's

my hope that as a teacher-servant to the families and children of Woodland Park, that I avoid the kind of top-down curriculum I decry. I see my role in our play-based curriculum not as the arbiter of what the children ought to learn or by when, but rather as an administrator of invitations to explore. Most of us in the preschool world are familiar with the idea of viewing art as a "process" rather than a "product," and I strive for this to hold true for everything we do. I provide materials, information, circumstances, challenges, and sometimes even examples, but so long as the children stay within the confines of the rules that we've agreed upon together, *what*, or even *if*, they learn is entirely up to them as individuals and as a community.

This leads often to a messy, noisy process, one that "borders on" or appears to be "controlled" chaos, but just as often it results in a circle of small heads bent over a single shared mote, discussing minutiae. That's what democracy always looks like, whatever our age.

In fact, democracy, when it functions as it should, is itself a play-based learning process, one in which we all engage in or not, bringing our own wisdom, knowledge, perspectives, and temperaments to the table. And together, through the process, we can be counted on to set things right, chaotically perhaps, slowly perhaps, difficultly perhaps, but without rebellion.

I am proud when civil disobedience emerges in my own classroom, times when the children have risen up against me as I attempt to impose my will upon them against theirs. People outside the progressive education bubble very often envision our school as an out-of-control, law-of-the-jungle kind of place, a Hobbesian dystopia, but that is not how it plays out, unless, of course, I chose to not listen to the will of the people. And then it is not the children who are subject to correction, but me. When I, for instance, attempt to hold the children at circle time beyond their attention spans or patience, the "rabble" lets me know it, first on the fringes as children begin to squirm and fidget. I know it is beginning to happen when I hear myself repeating things like, "I'd like you to sit on your bottom." When it's just one or two children, I may keep going forward with the things I've planned, things I hope we can explore together, but if my invitation doesn't compel the rest of them, if I've overstepped my authority and tried to make their bodies or minds do something for which they are not ready, if there is something else they would much rather be learning, I better wrap things up and move on unless I'm prepared to deal with a full-on rebellion.

This is not misbehavior. This is democracy. This is not a "problem" in our classroom, but rather an important part of how the children learn to be in charge of their own learning.

I don't know if we've yet reached the moment for civil disobedience when it comes to the corporate education reform. Maybe we can still afford to be "polite." Maybe there are still "proper channels" that need to be explored. Maybe there are hidden allies somewhere among our elected representatives who have listened and are preparing even as we speak to take a leading role. Maybe. Right now, however, I worry that we are being drowned out by the well-financed corporate reformers who control the microphone, that our objections are merely bouncing off the insides of our bubble, echoing back to us, creating the false illusion that the rabble is more roused than it is.

But every day—*every day*—I hear from parents or teachers who are angry, or desperate, or confused, people who know that schools can and should do so much better than turn a greasy profit and prepare children for corporate jobs; schools that "teach" the skills we know the future, and democracy, will demand: creativity, flexibility, resilience, motivation, and the ability to work with others. If it were my circle time, I'd be thinking about starting to wrap things up, but it's not. It's ours, and only we can decide what must happen next.

In the meantime, I will keep attempting to rabble rouse by teaching as I do and then writing about it.

When Democracy Suffers

I'm weary of hearing about "STEM," the popular acronym for "science, technology, engineering, and math." I'd be shocked if anyone reading here isn't aware of it being tossed around. Indeed, many of us have picked it up and held it high, declaring that play-based education is the perfect preparation for a career in STEM. Some of us have gotten clever and begun talking about STEAM education, tossing in "art" by way of expanding the notion, but it's a poor fit because "art" is not a career path the way the others are.

We're right, of course. When children play, they are scientists: exploring, discovering, hypothesizing, experimenting, concluding. When children play, they are using the technology at hand, solving engineering problems, and engaging in the sorting, organizing, and categorizing that forms the foundations of mathematics. All of that is true.

My objection is that all this talk about STEM is just the latest way to keep our schools focused exclusively on vocational training, to prepare our children for those mythological "jobs of tomorrow," jobs that may exist today but are unlikely to exist two decades from now when our preschoolers are seeking to enter the job market. It's a scam as old as public education, an idea that emerged from the Industrial Revolution because back then the "jobs of tomorrow" were stations along an assembly-line, where rote and repetition were king, so we made schools to prepare the next generation for that grim life. Today, those "jobs of tomorrow" are in cubicles, pushing buttons on computers, vocations that are equally prone to rote and repetition and equally likely to not exist in the future.

Most of the jobs my daughter will be applying for in the coming years didn't exist when she was in preschool. If I'd pursued the careers my guidance counselors recommended in high school, I'd be unemployed today. Anyone who claims to know the specific skills required for the jobs of tomorrow is just blowing smoke. They are wrong, and they have always been wrong. Those jobs of tomorrow, as is true in every generation, will instead be largely invented by the generation that fills them.

I did not enter the teaching game to prepare young children for their role in the economy, and if vocational training is the primary function of schools, then I'd say we ought to just shut them all down and let the corporations train their own damn workers. No, the purpose of education in a democracy ought to be to prepare children for their role as citizens, and that means that they learn to think for themselves, that they ask a lot of questions, that they question authority, that they stand up for what they believe in, and that they understand that their contribution to the world cannot be measured in money. The project of self-governance requires educated citizens, people who are self-motivated, who are sociable, and who work well with others. That is why I teach.

I'm married to the CEO of a technology company. She didn't study STEM in school. In fact, she admits to having steered clear of those classes, opting instead for a broad liberal arts education, one in which she pursued her passion for learning languages. Today, people invite her, as a one of those rare unicorns, "a woman in STEM," to speak with young people about her career. She is rarely invited back because she doesn't tell the kids what their teachers want them to hear. Instead, she tells them the truth, which is that her success is based on being self-motivated, being sociable, and working well with others.

Being able to earn a living is important, and none of this is to say that children ought not pursue their STEM interests, whether they lead to a career or not. But these things cannot stand at the center of education, and when they do, democracy suffers.

"You Just Teach Silly Things"

He said, "Teacher Tom, you should teach us things. You never teach us anything, just silly things."

I answered, "What do you mean? I teach you stuff all the time."

"No, you don't. You just teach us silly things."

"Okay, so what do you want me to teach you about?"

"I don't know."

This is a boy who enjoys knowing things. He has previously informed us that he knows everything about spiders, likewise volcanoes, and has followed that up by lecturing us with his impressive store of knowledge. Every preschool classroom has children like this, those who pursue their narrow passions, absorbing everything they can comprehend through the repeated watching of videos and library books and asking questions. It's self-directed learning at its most obvious.

Of course, every child is in the process of learning "everything" about something; it's just that their passions don't always fall so nicely into one of the "academic" categories like biology or geology. Some, for instance, might be going deep on their friendship skills or drawing the perfect butterfly or *Star Wars*. And some simply aren't specialists in life, at least not yet, opting instead, as my own daughter did to be more of a generalist, dabbling in lots of different pots, exploring the breadth of the world instead of its depth. That's also what self-directed learning is about.

I said, "Okay, how about I teach you everything about trees?"

"No."

"Then I could teach you everything about buildings."

"No."

"What about cheetahs?"

"No."

By now he was grinning as if he had suddenly understood a joke I was telling, as if he somehow realized that it was up to him, not me, to pick the subject, and that I was being silly yet again in even suggesting otherwise.

"Tell you what, when you think of something you want me to teach you, just tell me and I'll teach you."

"No, *I'll* teach me! You just teach silly things."

I Worry About "Loose Parts"

I suppose I'm happy that the concept of loose-parts play has taken the early childhood world by storm these past few years. It seems like not a day goes by that I don't discover a website dedicated to loose-parts play or a loose-parts workshop for teachers or a new book that will help us better understand it. Of course, it's an idea that's been around since the advent of children, one that was once just implied in the standard understanding of play. When left to their own devices, kids tend to pick up whatever is at hand and goof around with it. Then, over the course of modernization and commercialization, we came to understand the idea of "toys" manufactured specifically for children's play, and many of us adopted those things as the hub around which play necessarily revolved.

Children, of course, still continued to play with loose parts, some of which were these toys, broken, modified, or otherwise, but we adults lost sight of that amidst the bright colors, flashing lights, and annoying noises of those objects that came from toy stores. And as toys became cheaper and more prevalent and better marketed, our homes and classrooms have come to be overwhelmed with them. But even then, children continued their loose-parts play. Who among us, for instance, hasn't joked that our kids prefer the boxes the toys came in over the toys themselves?

So yes, I'm pleased that there is a renewed focus on the open-endedness of things like rocks and sticks and pinecones, of toilet paper tubes and mint tins and yogurt containers, of old tires and planks of wood and house gutters, but I worry that we are on the edge of turning those into just another commodity to be bought and sold. I worry that in our embrace of loose-parts play we are concentrating far too much on the loose parts and not enough on the play. I worry when I hear teachers fussing about their "loose parts" collection, hovering over the children lest they damage or misuse or lose their precious loose parts.

The children at Woodland Park have been engaged in loose-parts play for as long as I've been the teacher there, but you'll rarely hear me use the term. I usually just call it "junk," or in the case of items that come from nature like leaves or sticks, I might refer to it as "debris." Whatever it's called, the key element is that we didn't pay for it, and I have no concerns that it will be damaged, misused, or lost. Most of what you'll find on our playground came either from the earth itself or from the garages, attics, and recycling bins of the families who have enrolled their children. I often say that one of the functions of preschools isn't to use stuff, but to *finish* using it. We still have toys around, but most of them are broken in some way—the cars have lost wheels, the dolls have lost their heads, and the balls have lost their shape. When we do spend money, it's not on toys or loose parts, but rather on tools and furniture, things that need to be sturdy.

So while I'm pleased that more and more of us are discussing the value of loose-parts play, I guess my caution is that we don't lose sight of the fact that you don't need to go shopping for these things and you don't need to "teach" the children how to play with them. Your world is already abundant with loose parts. Your recycling bin is full of them, your cellar is choc-a-bloc, and a broken toy is often much better than a new one. Our main job is to simply make junk available and to step out of the way. The kids, as they always have, know what to do with it.

They're Talking about Rote

The opposite of play isn't work, it's rote. ~Edward Hollowell

This might sound like an odd thing for a teacher to write, but I sometimes get the idea that knowing stuff is the enemy of education. There is little gratification in it for me when I've envisioned how children will do something, then they proceed to do it in just the way I've imagined. Certainly, I could claim it as some evidence of experience on my side, but it also makes me worry that it's also evidence of rote on the children's side.

I'll leave it to future teachers to worry about teaching the kids to follow instructions if that's what they feel they need them to do. Much better things are happening in our school, it seems, when instructions are minimal, and I'm constantly proven wrong in my expectations. Fortunately, when working with young children in a play-based environment, that's more the norm than the exception.

Our classroom, every day, should be one big experiment, a place where things are *not* known by either the kids or the teachers, a place where we fiddle and argue and poke and prod our way *toward* knowledge, and where everything we come to understand is only a part of all the other things we're striving to know. It should be a place with lots of room for failure, frustration, and conflict. It should be a place with lots of room for wonder, epiphany, and friendship.

When a reporter asked Thomas Edison how it felt to have failed over a thousand times in his quest to invent the lightbulb, he famously answered, "I didn't fail a thousand times. The lightbulb was an invention with a thousand steps." Except we're not even trying to invent anything here, but simply discover, in the spirit of pure science, conducted for the purpose of getting closer to our own truth and nothing more.

Or maybe we *are* trying to invent something, after all, and if we are, it's not the sort of thing that can be put into words, but rather felt or intuited. I suppose it has something to do with inventing ourselves both as individuals and as a community. It's something that can only be invented by conducting thousands and thousands of experiments, by taking thousands and thousands of steps.

And even though billions of humans have come before us, if we are playing together, we are discovering and inventing a thing that has never been discovered or invented before: *us*.

Anyone who tells you they have a system or method or sure-fire technique for educating children isn't talking about education at all. They're talking about standardization and efficiency. They're talking about assembly lines and cookie cutters. Anyone who doesn't start with the idea that it's all an experiment isn't talking about education at all. They're talking about rote.

Marching in a Line

Several years ago, we took what was then our class on a field trip to the Ballard post office. The woman showing us around greeted us in the lobby, introduced herself, then before inviting us behind the scenes, asked the children to form a line and follow her.

As our parent chaperones did what they could to coax and cajole the children into something resembling a line, I explained to her, "We've never walked in a line before." I could tell she was slightly appalled at this notion. After all, wasn't this one of the fundamental "school skills?" There were moments when we managed a half dozen kids in a row, but by the time we'd wrangled the rest into place, the early adopters would grow restless and dart off to mess with the water fountain or peek into the little windows on the PO boxes. And, as I would have predicted, several of the children outright rebelled at the idea, crying and otherwise fighting any attempt to force them to stand in a certain place, facing a certain direction.

Our guide was growing frustrated, so I finally resorted to asking each chaperone to take the hands of two kids each, then for the adults themselves to form a queue. I said to our host apologetically, "This is the best we're going to do," and so that's how we started the field trip, a ridiculous, raggedy line of adults marching in line with kids in tow. It was a circumstance that lasted until we passed into the back room where the adults themselves lost their discipline, and our host, resigned to working with savages, struggled to remain pleasant through her tight lips.

I understand that there might be circumstances in

which my fellow teachers might find walking in a line is necessary. After all, they are often without all those extra adults in the form of parents that we enjoy in a cooperative school. It's a way to get kids to be responsible for their own safety when out in public, I suppose, but I have never found the need around the school. And indeed, when I ask myself why young children are routinely expected to queue up to march around their own school hallways, while transitioning from room-to-room, for instance, I can't think of a reason beyond "discipline."

Soldiers march about in lines, obeying the commands of superiors, but as a citizen in a democratic society, like the one we seek to create at Woodland Park, like the one we seek to create in our nation, learning to obey simply for the purpose of learning to obey, flies in the face of what self-governance is all about. And that's what this sort of line-walking discipline is all about: obedience, an anti-democratic stand-in for the important life skill of self-discipline, and that comes from within, not without, always. There is no overlap.

I was secretly cheered by the fact that not even our Woodland Park parents could maintain the post office marching formation for more than a few minutes, just as I was proud of the children who refused to be told where to stand. Those are the kinds of citizens alongside whom I want to self-govern, and those are the kinds of citizens into which I hope the children I teach grow.

I Will Not Permit Children, My Friends, to be Turned over to Machines

"Sometimes you want to go where everybody knows
your name, and they're always glad you came."
~*Cheers* Theme Song

I typically wait by the door or gate to greet the children as they arrive. *"Hi Sarah! I'm happy to see you!"* I say it because it's how I would like to be greeted. In a way, I guess, you could consider it my version of shouting, "Norm!" the way the *Cheers* regulars did each time their beloved friend walked through the door.

I also say it because it's true. I am happy to see each child walk through the door. I'm grateful they've come back. I'm grateful that their parents continue to trust me with their babies. I'm grateful that we are going to now spend hours together, just farting around, making stuff, imagining stuff, thinking about stuff, and generally just goofing off. I'm even grateful for the times we get sad or angry, because those conflicts are a part of our friendship.

And that's the thing, that's the part that people who don't do this job will never understand: the friendship. These kids are my friends, especially those who are back for a second or third year with me. We finish each other's sentences and crack inside jokes. This is what I will remember from the too-short time we spend together. It is also what they will remember.

There are those who predict that "extraordinarily inspirational" robots will be replacing teachers within the next decade. Not only do I hope they are wrong, I expect that reality will prove the whole idea a disaster, but we won't *know* until real damage has been done to real children who will be guinea pigs in an experiment where they won't have a friend like me at school, but rather a machine that pretends.

For instance, a California school district recently told parents that their child would no longer have a teacher. Instead, the district had invested in an "exciting new way of learning"—a "personalized learning program" called Summit, designed by Facebook.

That's a lot like having a robot for a teacher. If I were one of those parents, I'd be running like the wind. Inspiration, no matter how extraordinary, is a poor substitute for love and friendship.

Come on, really? Are we that stupid? People *need* other people, not just for procreation or telling stories or being happy or forming a team, but also for learning *anything* worth learning. We will figure out how to read and write and cipher as we always have: virally, by hanging out with other people, which is a system that has worked for most people throughout history. It's been a largely successful system, so why the hell would we mess with it? And that's also, not incidentally, how we learn everything else: virally, by hanging out with other people. And that requires friendship, deep-down, real friendship. That, ultimately, is the source of extraordinary motivation.

Read Summit's own documents, they admit that they are planning to turn live, face-to-face teaching into a "premium service," meaning that they know face-to-face instruction is a better way to learn, and they have no intention of having their own children learn from machines.

As ridiculous as it is, I am not laughing about these predictions. I'm girding myself because billionaires are behind this, and they, despite their philanthropic BS, care primarily about making a killing at the expense of our kids. I will not permit children, my friends, to be turned over to machines. I want them to come to a place where everybody knows their names and where they're always glad they came.

Even If I Don't Wear Nylons and Heels

At a backyard barbecue one afternoon, an older woman, her own children close to my age, not knowing anything about me or my profession, launched into a well-practiced monologue on what's wrong with kids these days, the centerpiece being that they are no longer taught to respect anything or anyone. We've probably all heard this one before. One of the examples she gave of how we're letting the kids down was how sloppily teachers dress for school. In her day, the young women wore skirts or dresses, "nylons," and heels ("clunky heels, but heels").

I let her finish most of her piece, although stopped her from going into a full-on diatribe about how horrible teachers are by admitting that I'm a teacher myself, one who works in torn jeans and T-shirts. I then agreed that children aren't as respectful now as they were back in the olden days. This, I've learned, is one of the keys to "winning" these sorts of cocktail party disagreements: start by finding something with which you can agree, then give them something with which they can agree right back. Humans might like to disagree with one another when we're all sort of anonymous, but when we're face-to-face, most of us crave agreement. So I said, "Of course, respect is something you have to *earn* no matter how you dress."

"Oh, yes." She agreed with that wholeheartedly, echoing, "You have to *earn* respect." This was our starting point, then: kids aren't as respectful as they used to be, and that respect has to be earned.

I'd earlier learned that she had, that morning, been driven by one of her sons up to Seattle from Vancouver,

Washington, three hours to the south, where she had lived in the same house for over forty years, so I figured what I was about to say next would be something else with which she would readily identify: "I think one of the biggest problems is that too many kids are being raised without their grandparents around."

"When we were growing up," I continued, including her as a peer, "our parents could count on grandparents to help them out, or even aunts and uncles, but families today are so spread out. I think it leads to a lot of parents feeling isolated and alone with their kids, especially when they live in a suburb." I waved my hand to indicate the backyard in which we were sitting. "And then their spouses head off to work in the city each morning, leaving them all alone with the kids.

"What are they going to do? It's mom and children all day long. The kids grow up as the center of mommy's universe, so why wouldn't they grow up to believe everything revolves around them?" We then chatted back and forth about the value of multi-generational families, of how grandparents are always ready to jump in, of how twelve-year-old girls (cousins and older siblings) once served as mommy's helpers, and how vitally important it is for kids to be loved by as many people as possible.

We were nodding and agreeing by this time, kindred spirits. That's when I said, "I feel sorry for these moms who don't have their extended families around. So many of them don't have a proper support system. They never get time for themselves, and many of them don't even realize how much they deserve it. They think that's what being a parent has to be: always putting their needs *after* their children's. Kids notice everything. They come to believe that this is the way it's supposed to be. It's hard to learn to respect others when you've learned that your needs always come first."

She got it. "Exactly!"

"My wife and I were lucky to have two sets of grandparents within twenty minutes of our home. They were always willing to watch their grandkid for a few hours or a weekend or a week. Not only is it great for the kids to spend time with other adults who love them, but it shows them that sometimes mommy comes first. I think that's what we're talking about. We want kids to learn respect, but it's a two-way street. When we were young, we tended err too much on the side of respecting the adults. Now maybe we err too much on the side of respecting the kids. We're all human beings here: we're all worthy of respect, and it starts with respecting ourselves.

"At school, the kids know that sometimes their needs come first, but just as often, mine do, too. I respect them and they respect me. Sometimes we do what they want to do, and sometimes we do what I want to do. I think that's the only way anyone has ever earned respect."

"Exactly!" she said again. By now, she was entirely on my bandwagon, so I huddled up with her, we two thoughtful people out there in lawn chairs, and in a conspiratorial tone, said, "You know what drives me crazy? Obedient kids, because they grow into obedient adults."

She chuckled with me. "Don't I know it."

"I want kids to question my authority. I want them to challenge me." I was now talking about the opposite of the kind of "respect" about which she had originally spoken. I told her about how I teach kids to think for themselves, how I don't want them to take my word for anything I can't prove, how our school trusts kids to make their own rules, how our whole democracy would be better off if we raised our kids to be rabble rousers. By the time we were done, she had, at least for the purposes of our backyard party conversation, *always* been an advocate for a progressive, play-based education, and a parenting style of mutual respect.

As we wound up our conversation, I said, "I guess if you want kids to show respect, you have to respect them." Then I left her with my favorite James Baldwin quote: "Children have never been very good at listening to their elders, but they have never failed to imitate them."

She said, "I'm glad to know there are still teachers like you. It gives me hope for the future."

She laughed when I replied, "Even if I don't wear nylons and heels?"

"Okay, Now Pretend to Roast Me for Dinner"

Three girls were playing together on our outdoor stage. I approached just as a fourth girl asked them, "Can I play with you?"

This is tricky question to ask around a preschool because the knee-jerk answer is most often no. Normally, I advise kids struggling to enter into an established play group to start by asking, "What are you playing?" or to state, "I'm going to play with you," or best of all, to simply drop to your knees and start playing. It still doesn't always work, of course, but I've noticed that kids who approach others like this are far more likely to have success.

In this case, however, one of the girls answered, "Sure, if you want to be an evil unicorn."

"I'll be an evil unicorn."

The girls then continued where they left off, with both the newcomer and me listening on.

"Okay, pretend I'm on the bridge and you come along and push me off."

From what I could gather, the girl asking to be pushed off was a good unicorn. For the most part, she was directing the evil unicorns in how to torment her. They pretended to push her off the planks of wood they had arranged as a bridge, then she said, "Okay, now pretend you're going to roast me for dinner."

There was an old bicycle tire on the stage. The good unicorn knelt down in it. One of the evil unicorns held a couple florist marbles. She put them on the good unicorn's back, saying, "These are so you'll taste better when we eat you."

"I'm already going to taste good."

"Yes, you will, dearie, but these jewels will make you taste even better."

The evil unicorns went through some motions around their roast while the newest evil unicorn looked on, still studying the game before leaping in.

After a few seconds, the roast popped up. "I'm done now. Now you have to wash me off." She retrieved a faucet set up (a spigot with hot and cold knobs mounted on a board) that had somehow appeared on the playground. The evil unicorns used it like a hose. Then the good unicorn said, "Pretend the bridge is the table and you're going to slice me up." She walked out on the bridge again and curled up under the spigot, repeating, "Now slice me up for dinner, dearie."

At first, the good unicorns used the sides of their hands to pantomime slicing, then one of them said, "Pretend I'm going to slice you with my staff," referring to the large stick she had been wielding.

They were interrupted by the newcomer calling out, "I don't want to be an evil unicorn. I want to be a good unicorn!"

"Okay, if you're a good unicorn, then we're going to have to roast you for dinner. Get in the oven." The newly be-monikered good unicorn dutifully took her spot within the circle of the bicycle tire.

"But first you have to eat me," insisted the other good unicorn.

"Don't worry, dearie, we'll eat you first."

Then the newest good unicorn called out, "And eat me too!"

"Of course, dearie, of course."

(Fairy tales) tell children what they unconsciously know—that human nature is not innately good, that conflict is real, that life is harsh before it is happy—and thereby reassure them about their own fears and their own sense of self.
~Arthur Schlesinger

"Teacher Tom, Ask Me a Question"

He approached me, his arms crossed, brow low. "Teacher Tom, ask me a question."

For the most part, I strive to ask the children I teach very few questions. Or rather, when I ask them questions, I want them to be real questions, ones to which I don't already know the answer, instead of the sorts of testing or rhetorical or otherwise stupid questions adults most frequently ask around schools. So I decided to go (mostly) with the big ones.

"When is the first day of the rest of your life?"

"Elephant."

"What is the meaning of life?"

"Ninjas."

"Who is the best baseball player?"

"Ichiro."

"What is the best color?"

"All of them."

"Rainbow?"

"No, all of them."

"Who is the most important person?"

"All of them."

"What is the most important time?"

"Snack time."

"What is the most important thing to do?"

"Wake up."

"Why do you want me to ask you questions?"

"So you will have answers."

And now I do.

Telling the Story of Right Now

I was sitting on a table near the entry to our playground. It's a spot at the top of the hill that forms our outdoor space and serves as a nice perch from which to observe the entire playground. Usually, I try to just observe, to make a study of my fellow humans.

A two-year-old came up to look at me, perhaps to make a study of me, not smiling, not talking. I smiled at her but echoed her wordlessness. She then went to sit on a nearby flight of stairs. I began to tell her story aloud.

"Carly is sitting on the stairs." She stood up. "Carly is standing on the stairs." She sat down. "Carly is sitting on the stairs."

We did this for a few cycles. Soon, as always happens when we start narrating the stories around us, a couple of other kids wanted to also be protagonists in the story of right now.

"Teri and Sylvia and Carly are sitting on the stairs."

"Teri is standing up. Sylvia and Carly are still sitting."

"Now Sylvia and Carly are standing up."

"Now Teri and Sylvia and Carly are all standing up. They are all smiling."

The girls turned to one another, smiling.

We did this for a while, with the girls delighting in the story they were making together. They began to lie down on the stairs. I said, "Sylvia is lying on the stairs. Teri is lying on the stairs. Carly is lying on the stairs. All of the girls are lying on the stairs."

They giggled together, then stood up, then sat down, then lay down once more as I told their story. Others began to join us. Before long, we were a story with a half dozen characters and almost as many observers.

Some of them started running down the hill and back. Others began to sit or lie or stand in other places: on the ground, on the wheelbarrow handles, on a pile of wood chips. I told the story as I saw it unfolding, sticking as strictly as I could to observable facts, describing what their bodies were doing, using their names, and describing their expressions. They sometimes looked at me, but mostly they made studies of one another, their fellow humans.

We "experts" usually call it "sportscasting" or "narrating," and I use those terms as well, but most of the time, I just think of it as telling the story of the children as they create it. It's not my story or your story; it's our story, and it's the story of right now.

Part Four:
Loving Them
Just As They Are

"You Just Have to Eat It"

The two-year-old said to me, "If you eat this food, you can have some ice cream." She placed a plate in front of me on which she had positioned a glob of purple play-dough.

I said, "What is it?"

"It's healthy food."

"What kind of healthy food."

"You just have to eat it."

"I'll need a fork."

"I'll get one for you, Teacher Tom." She dug around on the shelf until she found a plastic one. "Here's your fork, now eat your food."

I pretended to take a bite. Sometimes when kids want me to taste their imaginary food, I make a comical face and say, "It's yucky," or "It's too hot!" but this time I said, "That is so good! I'm going to eat it all!" I stabbed the play-dough with my fork, pretending to shove the whole thing in my mouth, then hid it on my lap while mimicking chewing and swallowing. "Now I'm ready for my ice cream."

The "ice cream" was more play-dough she held in a container. For a moment, I thought she was going to serve it to me, but then she said, "First you have to take your bath, then you can have some ice cream."

"I don't want to take a bath."

"You have to take a bath if want to have some ice cream."

"I'll need a wash cloth."

"I'll get one for you, Teacher Tom." She found a small blanket in our cradle of baby dolls. "Here's your wash cloth."

I mimed bathing, then said, "All clean and fresh. Now I'm ready for that ice cream."

"No, first you have to put on your jammies."

"I don't want to put on my jammies."

"You have to put on your jammies, then you can have some ice cream."

It went on for a couple more rounds like this. It was clear that I wasn't going to get any ice cream.

It was all pretend. The food wasn't real, the bath wasn't real, the pajamas weren't real. Even the ice cream wasn't real. Nothing about this was real, it was all a child's game, yet as she dangled that reward always just out of reach, I found a thread of growing annoyance and helplessness underneath my play. I felt manipulated and controlled. I'd jumped through her hoops, yet there was always another placed before me. The game was pretend, but the emotions it evoked were real.

Just think how much stronger those emotions would be were I the child, she the adult, and it was not a game, but rather a part of my day-to-day reality.

Your Child Is a Creative Genius

Every parent I've ever met knows her child is a creative genius. Sometimes they come right out and say it, but most often I see it in their sense of awe as they share stories and anecdotes about their kids. Sure, they most often frame it as "cute," but you can see it in their faces, in the tone of their voices, in the wide-eyed enthusiasm with which they talk about their kids that they are genuinely impressed and even amazed. One of the best parts of my job as a teacher in a cooperative preschool, in fact, is that I'm not just surrounded by these genius kids, but also by their parents who tend to be "turned on" by their children's genius. And as they spend time in the classroom working alongside me as assistant teachers, they invariably get to know the other children and, in turn, become amazed by the creative genius of not just their own child, but all the children.

One could argue, of course, that this is just the parenting instinct at work. Certainly, they aren't all creative geniuses. Certainly, true genius is as rare among preschoolers as it is among adults, where it is found in a relatively small percentage of us. That may seem like the most likely explanation, but it's not, at least according scientists working for NASA who have found that a full 98 percent of the four- and five-year-olds they tested fell into the category of "creative genius," while only 2 percent of adults do. And lest you think that this is just an isolated incident, the results have been replicated over and over again.

Sadly, these scientists have also found through longitudinal research that the percentage of creative geniuses falls to 30 percent by the time the kids are ten, 12 percent at fifteen, and a mere 2 percent among adults. The scientists who performed the research assert that it doesn't have to be that way, that virtually all of us could go through life as creative geniuses, but that our abilities have been systematically deadened by traditional schooling. I won't go that far. I believe there is something about the structure of society at large that tends to dumb us down with or without schooling, but it's something worth thinking about.

From the time I was a young man, I've always said that I didn't care how I spent my days just so long as I got to spend my time amongst "great brains." I did my time in academia and business, but it wasn't until I discovered my own child's genius that I realized that preschool is where the geniuses really are and that, perhaps more than anything else, is why I've stayed.

What to Say Instead of Commanding "Be Careful"

A parent once told me she thinks I'm like Roald Dahl's character Willy Wonka. "You always tell the kids, 'If you want to get hurt, go ahead and try it.'"

I do say those kinds of things. I once told a kid, "Hey, you could try sticking your finger in that electrical outlet!" He'd responded, "No, Teacher Tom, I might die!" At least once every field trip, I'll ask something like, "Should we run out in the street?" I know I can count on someone to remind me, "No, Teacher Tom, we'll get hit by a car!"

And yes, sometimes, when kids are apparently bent on attempting a feat that looks particularly hazardous, I'll say something along the lines of, "I'm going to watch to see who gets hurt so I know who I'm going to take care of while they're crying." To which the reply is, "Neither of us is going to get hurt because we're being careful."

If a couple of boys are racing our wagons down the hill, I might ask, "Hey, are you guys planning on running over anybody?"

And they'll answer, "No, Teacher Tom, because we're looking where we're going."

If someone is on the tire swing, I might suggest, "Hey, swing that direction and see if you can hit your head on the tree."

And they'll answer, "No, Teacher Tom, that would hurt."

If a couple of girls are using our homemade ladder to climb onto our monkey-bars climber, I might say, "Which one of you is going to fall?"

And they'll answer, "No, Teacher Tom, we won't fall, because we're holding on!"

Or if children making a yarn spider web start wrapping it instead around their necks, I'll say, "If you don't want to breathe anymore, you can put a whole lot more around your neck."

And they'll answer, "No, Teacher Tom, I want to breathe!"

I guess it's what I do instead of commanding, "Be careful!"

I do not make these comments sarcastically (as it might seem here on paper), but rather either as earnestly as possible or as obvious jokes.

In *Charlie and the Chocolate Factory*, the children did not fare too well. As a boy, I recall feeling that they were all, with the exception of Charlie, quite stupid for acting with no consideration of the possible consequences. As an adult, I now see Dahl's larger point: their stupidity was the consequence of bad parenting.

But that's fiction. In the real world, young children are capable of assessing many of their own day-to-day risks, but only if they've had the chance to practice; only if they're well versed in the art of critical thinking and not the habits of mere obedience. An adult who commands, "Don't slide down that banister!" might be keeping a child safe in that moment, but is also, at the same time, robbing him of a chance to think for himself, which makes him that much less safe in the future when no one is there to tell him what to do. Better to state the facts ("If you slide down that banister, you might get hurt.") and let him practice thinking things through for himself, to consider the possible consequences of his actions, to assess his own risks, to ask himself, "Is this a risk worth taking?"

There are no guarantees, of course, but the habit of critical thinking is, I think, the best safety precaution there is.

Loving Them Just As They Are

I have spent my adult life trying to figure out why parents and society put themselves into a race—what's the hurry? I keep trying to convey the pleasure every parent and teacher could feel while observing, appreciating and enjoying what the infant is doing. This attitude would change our educational climate from worry to joy. ~Magda Gerber

It seems to me that the greatest gift we can give to other people is to let them know we love them just as they are. That we've all heard this before in some version or other makes it no less profound and no less precious.

I think that's what we do when we simply let ourselves *be* with young children, without that sense of possession or protectiveness or responsibility that too often attends our interactions. It's in those moments of two humans simply being together that we convey this vital knowledge of unwavering love to even the youngest children, who themselves are then permitted to *be*, without the obligations that come with being possessed, protected, or a responsibility.

I'm grateful to such guides as Janet Lansbury, who continues to educate me about the ideas of Magda Gerber, and it's this idea of sincerely and carefully observing (what I think I have previously understood incompletely as "waiting") that resonates the most with me. But this observation is an essentially academic act, I think, without our own appreciation and joy in what the infant is doing or what we are doing together. Not only do we ourselves come to a deeper understanding of the child, but it's only through this heartfelt appreciation and joy that we actually convey to children the unconditional love that is our gift.

It may seem strange, I suppose, for many of us to understand that we, at best, stand on the planet as equals with *all* the other people, including young children. We are each fully formed, fully valid, fully functional human beings, no matter our age. Naturally, we have different lots in life, different blessings and challenges, and are on our way to different places, but we always remain, most of all, worthy of being loved for being exactly who we are.

Parents and teachers traditionally see our role as helpers, instructors, or guides, agents for moving young children through the world from point A to point B along their developmental track, ticking off milestones in baby books or report cards like we might a shopping list, taking pride in each "accomplishment." We can't help but look ahead, anticipating the next destination, worrying about the next bumpy patch, feeling guilty about our failings when we lose our way or fall behind schedule. It makes us impatient, lead-footed, prone to live outside the present moment as we move relentlessly toward a future. We forget to just *be* with our children as they are right now. That future child does not exist: *this* is the real child, the one before you right now, and she is perfect.

We are, in fact, at our best when we manage to successfully override those urges to help, instruct, or otherwise guide a young person, and instead give him the space and time to struggle, to practice, to come to his own conclusions. This, not our superior experience or intellect, is the great gift we have to give to children: to stop, to really see who they are right now, and *be* with them in appreciation and joy, loving them just as they are.

The More Time Your Children Spend Outside, The Smarter They Will Be

At the beginning of the 2015 school year, Seattle's public school teachers were on strike. They had a list of demands, most of which were ultimately met, including the requirement that all elementary school children receive a minimum of thirty minutes a day on the playground. As pathetic as that victory might sound to those of us who live and work in the world of play-based education, some schools were limiting their charges to fifteen minutes of recess over a school day. This is not an uncommon phenomenon in America and indeed many other parts of the world.

As heartlessly cruel as this sounds, it's the result of administrators and teachers who have bought into the entirely unsupported myth that more "instruction time" will result in "better results," and that every moment of free play, especially outdoors, is a waste of time. Meanwhile, 17 million children worldwide have been prescribed addictive stimulants (like Ritalin), antidepressants, and other mind-altering drugs for "educational" and behavioral problems, over half of them in the US. Already, one in ten American students are on these drugs, and the fastest growing segment are *children five and under*.

From the *Independent*:

> Tests to assess...children's physical development at the start of the first school year found that almost a third to be "of concern" for lack of motor skills and reflexes. Almost 90 per cent of children

demonstrated some degree of movement difficulty for their age…The tests suggest up to 30 per cent of children are starting school with symptoms typically associated with dyslexia, dyspraxia, and ADHD—conditions which can be improved with correct levels of physical activity, experts say.

What's to blame? Lack of physical play is a big part of it, but there's more. According researcher Dr. Rebecca Duncombe:

> "Young children have access to iPads and are much more likely to be sat in car seats or chairs… But the problem can also be attributed to competitive parenting—parents who want their children to walk as soon as possible risk letting them miss out on key mobility developments which help a child to find their strength and balance."

And why do we have competitive parenting: because our schools, indeed our entire educational environment, is built around the idea of competition; around the cruel caution that "You don't want your child to fall behind." Bill Gates and his ilk have succeeded in "unleashing powerful market forces" on our children, and this is the result. Because we have to get them ready for the "competitive job market of tomorrow," we've herded them indoors, where they spend their days locked in, being force-fed "knowledge" like it's some sort of factory farm. It's so bad that we have to drug them. It's so bad that 90 percent of our four-year-olds aren't even getting the opportunity to learn how to move their bodies properly. The only other human institutions of which I'm aware that regularly drug and confine people are prisons and mental wards.

Instead of understanding the truth about young children—that they need to move their bodies, a lot, and preferably outdoors—we have created a very, very narrow range of "normal" into which we are forcing our children. This is outrageous. It's malpractice. And it's on all of us for letting it happen.

I usually try to end on a positive or hopeful note, but the best I can do right now is to say that at least Seattle's public school kids are getting their thirty minutes outdoors... Unless, of course, they are being punished, because taking away recess is one of the more common "consequences" for children who can't sit still and focus. And if they fail too often, we drug them.

Parents: the more time your child spends outdoors, playing, the smarter she will be. Create it at home and demand if from our schools. Teachers: the more time your students spend outdoors, playing, the smarter they will be. Create it at school and demand more of it from your administrators. This is the science. This is what we *know* about children. What's happening now is nothing short of institutionalized child abuse, and we're all a part of permitting it to happen.

"Teaching" Responsibility

"We hold these truths to be self-evident, that all men are created equal, that they are endowed by their Creator with certain unalienable Rights, that among these are Life, Liberty and the pursuit of Happiness."
~*Declaration of Independence*

There was a time when I started Tuesday afternoons by eating lunch with the oldest kids, each child bringing something from home to eat. I took note of their lunch boxes and bags as they arrived: "I see you have a fire fighter lunch box today," or "I'll bet you have sushi in that bag."

Often, a child arrived at the table without a lunch, and I'd ask, "Where's your lunch?"

"Mommy has it."

"Why does mommy have it? Is she going to eat it?"

"No, I'm going to eat it, Teacher Tom."

They thought I was clowning around, but I wasn't. I answered matter-of-factly, something like, "I carry my own lunch."

By the end of the school year, all of these kids would have assumed responsibility for carrying their own lunches, taking their lunch box from their mothers' hands of their own accord because that is simply what we did.

We all want our kids to be responsible: we want them to carry their own things, to dress themselves, to pick up after themselves. We nag them when they don't do those basic things we know they're capable of doing. Or maybe we're more sanguine, shrugging our shoulders and doing it for them, not up for the battle of wills this time. Still, we know they're going to have to learn it *sometime*. We see what's in store for them if they don't. We fear they'll show up in the world as some sort of entitled prima donna, going through life expecting others to do everything for them.

Even enlightened parents try rewards (e.g., if you get yourself dressed, you get hot chocolate) and punishments (e.g., if you don't pick up your coat, you won't get hot chocolate), and they can appear to work for a time, but the external nature of the motivation makes it a temporary fix, one that stops working the moment the reward or punishment isn't present. Some of us try the route of natural consequences, but who among us can abide a messy bedroom longer than a child? They easily outlast us, their standards being much lower, and besides, they possess the knowledge that Aunt Milly will soon visit and that Mom will do it for us in the flurry of housekeeping that always precedes the arrival of guests, often muttering something like, "This is the last time…"

A few Decembers back, I told people that the gift I most wanted was that they take a twenty-dollar bill, find the most unapologetic street person they could, and hand it to him with a cheery, "Merry Christmas!" fighting any temptation to place conditions on its expenditure. I'm certain that none of them, even my most liberal or most Christian friends, took me up on it. (And in the interest of full disclosure, I didn't do it myself.) Many of them asked, "Why would you want that? They'll just use it for booze." Most informed me that the money would do much more "good" if funneled through a responsible charity where it would get spent on things they need like food, clothing, and shelter.

Irresponsibility, the unwillingness to take responsibility for oneself, at least according to our own standards of what that means, be it a clean room or a clean and sober life, grates on us. When it's our own kids, we grudgingly do it for them, telling ourselves that "this is the last time." When it's an irresponsible adult, even the most noble of us hold back, not wanting to "encourage" them, thinking somehow that our twenty dollars will just perpetuate their bad choices, their profligate ways, their degeneracy.

It's what *we* want. And that's really the challenge: the conceit that we know best.

We live in a society of rights as well as responsibilities, and one of those rights is to not live up to other people's standards of responsibility. In our self-righteous quest to teach lessons, we forget that responsibilities, like rights, are not something we learn, but rather something we assume. And the two, rights and responsibilities, go hand in hand: they don't exist independently, but rather emerge from one another.

All of us, pauper or king, are born with the three rights asserted in the *Declaration of Independence*, in what I consider to be among the most perfect sentences ever written in the English language: life, liberty, and the pursuit of happiness.

"Life" has certain requirements that we are bound as parents and as a society to provide, among them food, clothing, and shelter. To that I would add such things as medical care, clean air, and physical touch. These are the rights every child already has to the degree that our families and society lives up to their promises, because to do otherwise is to deny this unalienable right.

"Liberty" is more challenging. Rightly or wrongly, our laws recognize an age (or *ages*, in the bizarre practice of granting voting rights at eighteen and drinking rights at twenty-one) at which his right of "liberty" is fully granted. This is equally challenging for parents, who with good reason fear their inexperienced child, if granted full liberty, will make dangerous, even life-threatening choices, so we must, for a time, limit it in the name of sustaining their first right of "life," at least until they're old enough to assume the full right of liberty. But at the end of the day, most of us are able to grant that *all adults*, whatever their station in life, have an equal amount of unalienable liberty.

It's through the right to pursue happiness that responsibilities emerge. This is the part of the promise of democracy in which we acknowledge that we must engage with one another, accommodate, share. School is the first place most of us get to practice this right and experience the responsibilities that go with it.

As I assume my right to pursue happiness within a community, for instance, I must also assume the responsibility of following its rules: not hitting or taking or screaming in someone else's ear. As I assume my rights, I also assume the responsibilities that come with community property, such as sharing or taking turns. As I assume my rights to freely play and explore, I also assume the responsibility to help clean up those things when it's time to move on to something else.

These are not things I assume because I've been nagged into it. I do not assume them because of some external reward or punishment. I take on those responsibilities because "that's what we do." Responsibilities are not the consequence of my pursuit; they are a part of my pursuit.

If my pursuit leads me to join a church, I take on the corresponding rights and responsibilities to live according to its creed.

If my pursuit requires me to have a job, I take on the corresponding rights and responsibilities of fulfilling its obligations.

If my pursuit causes me to have a family, start a charity,

organize a party, or buy a house, I also assume those rights and responsibilities.

If my pursuit requires me to stand on a street corner and panhandle, I may assume few responsibilities, but I also assume few extra rights beyond those that are unalienable. (For the sake of this argument, I understand that I've set aside the realities of homelessness and poverty, and am stipulating for a moment that living on the streets is a "choice.")

I've written often on the blog about how the children of Woodland Park, even our youngest members, take on the responsibility of cleaning up the classroom. Each time I do, people write me, asking what I do about the kids who "refuse" to help. And it's true, there are always on any given day, a few kids who opt out altogether. What I do about them is nothing other than to *not* allow them to interfere with the community project of clean-up. I say, "We're putting that away," when they continue their play. I say, "That is closed," when they try to get out a new toy. I reply, "We're cleaning up now," when they try to engage me in conversation. You see, participating in clean-up is one of the responsibilities that comes with the right of being a member of our community, and you simply are not a full member unless you take that on. It's what we do.

That still doesn't answer the question of how to get the kids to carry their own things, dress themselves, or pick up after themselves at home. But I do know that responsibilities are not things into which one is commanded or shamed, rewarded or punished: that's called obedience. Responsibility emerges only from the unalienable right to pursue happiness.

I am the parent of an adult now. I've noticed that the more rights she assumes, the more responsibly she behaves. That's what we do in a democracy.

"I Want to Know These Things!"

When our daughter Josephine was little, I decided to expose her to a little "culture" and rented the Disney movie *Snow White and the Seven Dwarfs*. It had been a long time since I'd seen it. My memories were of silly dwarfs, uplifting songs, and a handsome prince. I'd completely forgotten the frightening parts, especially the terrifying early scene where the Huntsman raises his knife to cut out the heroine's heart followed by her pell-mell escape through the dark and forbidding forest.

It overwhelmed Josephine. She demanded I turn the movie off, but then, to my confusion and surprise, a few minutes later, she asked me to show that part to her again. Then again. Then again. We must have watched that scene a dozen times or more before she permitted us to move on. It scared her, but at the same time compelled her enough to want to confront the fear and peer more deeply into that particular abyss.

Recently, an online group of parents and teachers were discussing a book called *The Amazing Bone* by the author William Steig. Now this is a book I've been reading to preschoolers since I discovered it nearly two decades ago, but most of the people in the group felt it was entirely inappropriate, even for older children. In particular, they found the folllwing page to be disturbing.

The illustrations show masked bandits attempting to rob poor Pearl at gun and knifepoint. The text reads: "You can't have my purse," she said, surprised at her own boldness. "What's in it?" said another robber, pointing his gun at Pearl's head.

It's a frightening scene, no doubt, one that annually prompts deep and meaningful classroom discussions, taking us into our darker places.

I understand the instinct to want to protect children from disturbing imagery, and I did it myself as a parent. For the first many viewings of *The Sound of Music*, for instance, I would declare "The End" just before the Nazis began to pursue the Von Trapp family. When, years later, Josephine discovered what I'd done, she chewed me out.

When she was six, she reacted even more strongly to learning that the catastrophe of 9/11 happened during her lifetime. We were approaching the hole in the ground where the World Trade Center towers had once stood. As I told the story, she angrily interrupted me, "You mean it happened since I've been alive? Why didn't you tell me?" I explained that she had been too little, just three years old. She scolded, "I want to know these things! I want you to tell me the truth about these things!"

It was a moment that changed me forever: my wee, innocent baby demanding truth. Up until then, I thought I'd been the epitome of an honest parent, never shying away from her questions, but that moment, a moment that occurred as we approached the scene, caused my own conceit of integrity to collapse within me.

I hadn't told her about it, I thought, because I hadn't wanted her to be afraid. And now not only was she afraid three years removed, but feeling betrayed by her own father. I'm just glad she had the fortitude or courage or whatever it was to call me on it. I don't want to ever again be in that position, not with my child, my wife, or anyone for that matter. It's one thing when the world is crap. It's another to make it crappier.

When we lie, either overtly or by omission, especially to a loved one, we might tell ourselves it's altruism, but at bottom, it's almost always an act of cowardice. It's us who don't want to face truth. When we say, "She's too young," we're really saying, *I'm not ready to face the pain or the shame or the fear.*

We skip pages in books. We fast-forward through the scary parts. We distract their gaze from road kill.

I'm not saying that we should, unsolicited, lay out the whole unvarnished horrible mess before them, if only because we don't need to. It will reveal itself to them soon enough. Our job is neither to distract their gaze nor draw their attention to it. It is rather, out of our love for them, to answer their questions, to speak the truth as we know it, and to say, "I don't know," when that's the truth.

What anchors our children is not a sense that the world is perfect. They already know it isn't. They have known it since their first pang of hunger. They don't need more happy endings. They need to know we love them enough to tell them the truth, and to accept their emotions, to hold them or talk to them or just be with them.

It's adults, not children, who worship the false idol of childhood innocence. It's only adults who don't want to grow up.

"That's Better Than Getting Dead"

For a couple years, one of our students had expressed intense fear about fire, a phobia that her parents told me was triggered by having witnessed a neighborhood house fire. When she was younger, even talk of fire would cause her to cry so inconsolably that we modified how we handled fire drills. As she got older, her fear evolved to include the prospect of her family dying in a fire, leaving her all alone. It was not a debilitating phobia, and generally speaking, she was a cheery, enthusiastic kid, but anytime the conversation turned to fire or firefighters or fire engines, as they do in preschool, she either requested that we change the subject or made herself scarce. I get it, of course, not the specific phobia, but phobias in general. My own daughter had one about crabs and other shellfish, something that's not easy to avoid in the Pacific Northwest. And naturally, I have my own phobias.

One day, I was sitting with a group of kids around the snack table, one of whom was this girl with the fire phobia. I was slightly shocked when, out of the blue, she told us, with a very sad face, "When there's a fire at my house, my mommy will die. My sister will die too. And also my dad."

I wanted to tell her that her house was not going to burn down, but my knowledge of her phobia stopped me. The very fact that she was discussing this without hysterics seemed to be a kind of positive step in the direction of facing her fears, even if her scenario was disturbing.

"I won't get dead because I will jump out of my window. I might get hurt. I might get a cut, or something. But," she added with a small nod, "that's better than getting dead." We all agreed with that. "I'll go to the neighbor's house, and then I'll go live with my grandma in California."

Her face was both sad and sincere as she finished. I recognized evidence of parental counsel in her words, something that was later confirmed by her father, although, the way kids do, she had made it her own. Despite the unmitigated tragedy of her story, it was clear that it brought her comfort knowing that there were concrete plans in place should her greatest fear be realized. I recognized right then that this is also what I do with my own phobias: imagine the worst case then plan for how I'll deal with it.

We sat in silence for a moment at the end of her story, each of us reflecting, until a boy said excitedly, "If you live with your grandma, that means you can have movie night *every night!*"

She looked at him wide-eyed, then squealed, "Yes!" And then everyone around the table cheered.

Our Catastrophic Imaginations

Awhile back, I was watching a boy playing under the swings as a classmate was swinging. It wasn't a particularly risky activity in my view. I mean, I was standing right there, taking pictures, discussing it with him, and it didn't set off any alarm bells for me in the moment, although after the fact, while going through the photos, it occurred to me that it was something that would be scuttled in other settings. My lack of concern probably stems from the fact that it's far from the first time this sort of thing has happened.

In fact, I think what caught my attention about it was that it was the first time I'd seen a kid do more than just lay there giggling. Of course, many schools have removed their swings altogether, so maybe the very existence of swings is shocking to some.

I imagine that in some dystopian future we'll become notorious for being the *only* school left with a swing set, let alone for not having a set of rules about how the kids can use them. That's because, in our six years with swings, since our move to our current location, we've not found a need for safety rules, because the kids, the ones that live in the world outside our catastrophic imaginations, haven't shown a particular propensity to hurt themselves or one another.

Oh, sure, they get hurt like all kids do, like all people, but most of the injuries don't come from what people call "risky play," but rather from day-to-day activities, things you would think children had mastered. For instance, the worst injury we've seen during my long tenure at Woodland Park came when a boy fell on his chin while walking on a flat, dry, linoleum floor. He needed a couple stitches. Another boy wound up with stitches when he fell while walking in the sandpit.

Increasingly, I find myself bristling when I hear folks talk about "risky play," even when it's framed positively. From my experience, this sort of play is objectively *not* risky, in the sense that those activities like swinging or climbing or playing with long sticks, those things that tend to wear the label of "risky" are more properly viewed as "safety play," because that's exactly what the kids are doing: practicing keeping themselves and others safe. It's almost as if they are engaging in their own self-correcting safety drills.

When a group of four- and five-year-olds load up our tire swing with junk, then work together to wind it up higher and higher, then, on the count of three, let it go, ducking away as they do it, creating distance between themselves and this rapidly spinning thing that they've learned is libel to release its contents in random directions, they are practicing keeping themselves and others safe. They don't need adults there telling them to "be careful" or to impose rules based on our fears because those things are so manifestly necessary to this sort of thing that they are an unspoken part of the play.

When children pick up long sticks and start employing them as light sabers, swinging them at one another, they are practicing keeping themselves and others safe. The safety is built into it.

When children wrestle, they are practicing caring for themselves and their friends.

When preschoolers are provided with carving tools and a pumpkin, they automatically include their own safety and that of others into their play. Adult warnings to "be careful" are redundant at best and, at worst, become focal points for rebellion (which, in turn, can lead to truly risky behavior) or a sense that the world is full of unperceived dangers that only the all-knowing adults can see (which, in turn, can lead to the sort of unspecified anxiety we see so much of these days). Every time we say, "Be careful," we express, quite clearly, our lack of faith in our children's judgment, which too often becomes the foundation of self-doubt.

The truth is that they already *are* being careful. The instinct for self-preservation is quite strong in humans. It's a pity that we feel we must teach them to live within our catastrophic imaginations.

Adults Hitting Kids

Surveys show that something like 70 percent of Americans believe that children, at least sometimes, deserve to be spanked. Just writing that sentence makes me sick to my stomach: all those big adults hitting kids. Even worse, some researchers tell us that over 90 percent of preschoolers are spanked by an adult at least once in any two-year span, and 30 percent of children one year old and under have been spanked. Who could hit a baby?

Spanking is hitting. Hitting is violence. Violence is morally wrong, and I believe that the US should join the forty-eight nations that have made spanking illegal.

I've had people shrug at my moral stance and insist that spanking "works," and I'm sure it does. There are lots of things that work that I will never try. If I disagree with you, shouting you down works, but wouldn't it be better if I engaged you in reasonable debate? If I need money, stealing works, but wouldn't it better if I worked to earn a higher income? If you're standing in my way, pushing you works, but wouldn't it be better to politely ask you to allow me to pass? Indeed, spanking may work, but there are better ways. They just take more effort.

Obviously, 70 percent of us do not share my point of view and believe it is not only acceptable, but even necessary, for full-grown adults to hit children. I also know that when I post about this one on my blog or elsewhere, I will spend my day reading comments from people who are adamant, even angry at me, for suggesting that they stop hitting children. They will say that spanking is not hitting, a hair-splitting argument that makes no sense to me. They will say that spanking is not a problem if done "with love," an argument that tells me that there are a lot of people who don't understand love. They will say that spanking is the only way to teach obedience, a goal that I've spent my entire professional life rejecting. They will say, "My parents spanked me, and I turned out okay," to which I will respond, "Are you sure? You hit children."

But beyond my moral stance, the research is quite clear: spanking does much more harm than good. According to Murray Straus, founder and co-director of the Family Research Lab and professor emeritus of sociology at the University of New Hampshire, who has brought together more than four decades of research in his book *The Primordial Violence*:

> Research shows that spanking corrects misbehavior. But it also shows that spanking does not work better than other modes of correction, such as time out, explaining, and depriving a child of privileges. Moreover, the research clearly shows that the gains from spanking come at a big cost. These include weakening the tie between children and parents and increasing the probability that the child will hit other children and their parents, and as adults, hit a dating or marital partner. Spanking also slows down mental development and lowers the probability of a child doing well in school…More than 100 studies have detailed these side effects of spanking, with more than 90 percent agreement among them. There is probably no other aspect of parenting and child behavior where the results are so consistent.

From where I sit, children have a fundamental human right to not be the victims of violence. When adults do it to other adults, we call it "assault." Spanking is a violent act that does real harm to both children and the wider society. And while we can continue debating the efficacy of time outs and other punishments, can't we at least stop hitting children?

Without Love, It's Worse Than Useless, It's Meaningless

When we enrolled our daughter Josephine in cooperative preschool, I explained how it worked to a friend, telling her that there was one professional teacher in the room and a dozen assistant teachers in the form of parents. She freaked out saying, "How can you let amateurs teach your child? I only want professional teachers near my child." She feared that the parents of other children would somehow damage her child's educational prospects. So while Josephine spent her three years in co-op, my friend's son attended a preschool in which parents were not even allowed into the classroom, not even to observe.

I could no more have made her decision than she could have, apparently, made mine. Even as a new parent who had no inkling that teaching was in my future, I knew I wanted to be there with Josephine as much as possible, and when I wasn't, I wanted her to be surrounded by the love of a community. I didn't care about her having a teacher who could teach her how to "read" or identify Norway on map before she was three, like some kind of circus trick, I wanted her to be in a place where she simply got to play with friends and be guided by loving neighbors.

The more I teach, the better I feel about my decision.

What parents may lack as pedagogues (and, indeed, many of them are masters) they more than make up for by bringing love into a co-op classroom. And as Mister Rogers puts it:

> Learning and loving go hand in hand. My grand-
> father was one of those people who loved to

live and loved to teach. Every time I was with him, he'd show me something about the world or something about myself that I hadn't even thought of yet. He'd help me find something wonderful in the smallest of things, and ever so carefully, he helped me understand the enormous worth of every human being. My grandfather was not a professional teacher, but the way he treated me (the way he loved me) and the things he did with me, served me as well as any teacher I've ever known.

My friend also thought that our co-op sounded too much like "play school." She wanted her child to go to "real school." Again, as a new parent, my thoughts on the subject were not well-enough formed to answer her with a logical argument (not that it would have done any good), but I just knew she was wrong. Today, I know that to undervalue the importance of play for young children is to make a tragic mistake. Frankly, I think that goes for older children and adults as well. The times in life when my mind has been the most shut down are those times when I felt compelled to do "work" prescribed by others. When I've been playing, however, even if dressed up as hard work, that's when I've learned the most about myself and the world.

Again, from Mister Rogers:

Play does seem to open up another part of the mind that is always there, but that, since childhood, may have become closed off and hard to reach. When we treat children's play as seriously as it deserves, we are helping them feel the joy that's to be found in the creative spirit. We're helping ourselves stay in touch with that spirit, too. It's the things we play with and the people who help us play that make a great difference in our lives.

It's love and play that form the foundation of a good education. Without that, the rest is worse than useless, it's meaningless.

Conclusion

The End of Teacher Tom's Second Book

Over the course of the last seventy years or so, our expectations of children have changed dramatically. In many ways, we perceive them as less competent. As a society, we have lowered our expectations about what they are capable of doing in the world. They no longer walk themselves to school. None of them carry pocketknives, and for that matter are kept far away from most tools. And even if you trust your own child to be home alone as you run a quick neighborhood errand, our wider society considers you neglectful because, of course, children younger than, say, about fifteen, are perpetually on the verge of stupidly killing themselves (or being killed by nameless, faceless others) if left for even the briefest moment without adult supervision. Or so our urban legends about childhood would have it. As a result, our children are growing up in a world scrubbed of risk, challenge, hurt feelings, and failure because, as we've come to believe, they are not capable of handling it.

At the same time, and perhaps partly as a result of this cultural paranoia, we've placed unreasonable expectations on our children, especially our youngest children, in the form of schooling. We are institutionalizing our children at younger and younger ages. They are spending more and more time in "school" and less and less time playing, while being subjected to greater and greater academic expectations. Today, more than 80 percent of kindergarten teachers expect five-year-olds to be reading. In 1998, that number was 30 percent, and in 1950, that number was approaching zero. The fact that our literacy rate hasn't budged over the past half century despite these developmentally inappropriate expectations tells us that our early literacy efforts, at best, have no impact. However, there is ample evidence that this phenomenon is taking a mental-health toll on our children, with one in five children between the ages of three and seventeen struggling with a diagnosable mental illness, mostly in the form of anxiety and depression, much of which can be linked to these pressures.

These dynamics represent bookends of fear that are crushing our youth. We're afraid they are going to be hurt, so we've dramatically restricted them. We're afraid of them falling behind, so we reign them to carts in academic coalmines. It's almost as if our greatest fear is childhood itself . . . or children, or liberty, or play.

From where I sit, the time for school is at an end. We have clearly reached a point of diminishing, dramatically diminishing, returns. For most children, most of the time, school is a place where they can be safely warehoused and made to nose the grindstone in a way that is contrary to what large majorities of scientists and psychologists tell us is appropriate. This is the same phenomenon we're seeing with environmental denialism. We, as a society, are so committed to our *habit* of schools that we struggle to even consider a world without them, the most common knee-jerk question being, "But without schools, what will the children do while their parents are off at work?"

It's a central question, a question about caring for the children more than about "education," an important question that has been answered in different ways by different societies throughout human history. Most prime-of-life adults have pretty much always worked productively in useful ways; this is nothing new in human evolution, and while birth mothers may have traditionally shouldered a somewhat larger share of the burden of child care, a substantial part was handled by the wider community, the village. Instead of ghettoizing child care into out-of-the-way, low-paying, low-prestige corners, most prior human civilizations have placed caring for the children at the center of life, creating communities in which children were included, in which caring for them was the responsibility of us all, and in which they were free to have a childhood, under the watchful eyes and loving hearts of grandparents, aunts, uncles, cousins, and neighbors. It's from living in a community that we learn what we most need to learn from a wide variety of adults and other children, the lessons of working together, of being personable, of asking a lot of questions, of taking responsibility, and, when ready, and not necessarily waiting until the arbitrary age of eighteen or twenty-one, to assume our own productive, useful work.

We are currently a long way from achieving anything like that vision, but it is nevertheless the way forward, not just for children, but for all of us. If this change is to happen, it won't come from up high, but rather must bubble up from us, from individuals choosing to place caring for our children at the center of our lives. Indeed, it's already happening with more and more parents opting for homeschooling, unschooling, cooperatives, and democratic free schools. There is a lot of irrational fear to overcome. There is a lot of science denialism to overcome. There are a lot of addictive habits to break. And there are economic realities that make it seem insurmountable. But we know what to do, and that is to create community, to find it, to nurture it. It can begin to happen in libraries and on playgrounds, in work places and nursing homes. It can begin in our schools and churches; where sports are played, where music is made, and where dancing is happening. It starts when we seek to make space for children *everywhere* that community is happening. It starts with learning to trust more people, including children, because trust is the greatest antidote to fear.

When we bring the children back into the center of our lives, we will once more have the kinds of communities in which we can all thrive, together.

About the Author

Tom "Teacher Tom" Hobson is an early childhood educator, international speaker, education consultant, teacher of teachers, parent educator, and author. He is best known, however, for his namesake blog *Teacher Tom's Blog,* where he has posted daily for over a decade, chronicling the life and times of his little preschool in the rain-soaked Pacific Northwest corner of the US. For nearly two decades, Teacher Tom was the sole employee of the Woodland Park Cooperative School, a parent-owned and operated school, knit together by Teacher Tom's democratic, progressive play-based pedagogy. Teacher Tom came into teaching through the backdoor, so to speak, having enrolled his own child in a cooperative preschool, where he began working daily in his daughter's classroom as an assistant teacher under the tutelage of veteran educators, although he'll be the first to tell you that most of what he learned came from the children themselves. When it was time for his daughter to move on, he "stayed behind." Today, Teacher Tom travels around the world (Greece, Iceland, Australia, China, Vietnam, New Zealand, Canada, UK, and across the US) sharing his views on early childhood education, play, and pedagogy.

Please visit *Teacher Tom's Blog*,

where he has posted daily since 2009,

chronicling the life and times of

his little preschool in the rain soaked

Pacific Northwest corner of the United States.

teachertomsblog.blogspot.com